Living in Your Sweet Spot

Living In Your Sweet Spot

A Practical Guide to Your Authentic Life

Dr. Pat Gibson

*BOOK*LOGIX®

Alpharetta, GA

For Z

It's choice—not chance—that determines your destiny.

–Jean Nidetch

Contents

Acknowledgments

To Z, for being the most amazing kid any parent could ever ask for. To Joey, Mary, Lynn, Donna, Susie, Debra, Julie, Myron, and Nikki, for their continual support, encouragement, truth, and love. To Donna, for creating beautiful artwork for the cover. To Paula, for her steadfast guidance and belief in me. To Kerri, for holding me to task. To Sophie, for all her help in managing our lives. To the publishing staff, Daren, Jessica, and Laura, for making this book a reality.

Introduction

Are you bored with how you are living your life? Have you resigned yourself to the belief that your life is what it is? Is there some part of you that believes you could probably live a better life, but you're sick of trying, failing, and having nothing change? If you picked up this book, there's a good chance you are searching for a way to live a life that is more joyful and in harmony with your true or authentic self. Living in your sweet spot is that amazing feeling when all the pieces of your life live in harmony with each other.

It's not that issues and problems don't arise; it is the knowing and feeling that you are on the right track, living the life you were meant to live, not the life someone else wants you to live. When you are out of your sweet spot, life tends to be more of a struggle than fun. Dynamic tension—the push and pull you feel in your decision-making—is a necessary and integral part of making change. As you become aware of what you do to get in your own way and let go of the need to judge it, this tension becomes more of a discovery than a struggle.

Living in Your Sweet Spot is designed to guide you to understand what you do that brings you closer to or further from your authentic self. It is about what you do to protect, avoid, delay, deny, or excuse not living your life to its fullest potential—what I like to call our mischief. It is the story that we tell ourselves (or others) about why we can't do or have the things that we want. Although mischief has a playful side, it has a sneaky side too. It's sometimes so sneaky we are unconscious to the fact that we are the ones who are preventing ourselves from having the very things we desire. This book is designed to help you to uncover your current M.O. that is preventing you from living your authentic life. It is also my desire that in learning to understand yourself at this level, you will prevent yourself from developing new patterns or defense mechanisms. Living as your authentic self is not an end to a journey, but a choice that evolves and changes each moment of every day.

There are a number of different things that keep people from living their dreams. For some, it is the inability to know what they want. Others are too busy living a hectic, stressed-out life to slow down and consider what life they are truly meant to live. Some don't feel worthy or deserving, and others believe they need to live or behave in a specific way to have the things they desire. It is critical to understand what you do to prevent yourself from living a life filled with passion, joy, and fun. We are all unique and incredibly creative in the ways we keep ourselves from this.

After thirty years of experience with patients, facilitating and developing workshops, and learning my own life lessons, this book offers you a comprehensive collection of tools and concepts that will bring you closer to understanding what your mischief is and how to change it. *Living in Your Sweet Spot* will provide you with all the information you need to stimulate, guide, and, hopefully, incite you to address the things in your life that have been holding you back from living the life you want.

Some things we already do really well in our lives, and for these things, there is no need to reinvent the wheel. Although I feel each chapter will offer you something, I suggest that you spend more time with the sections of the book that relate to concepts you struggle with and look for whatever nuggets you may find in the chapters that you are already fairly proficient with.

For example, if you live in a fairly buff, to-die-for body and eat really well but hate your job, dread most days at work, and long for the week-ends, you may want to check out the chapters on following the thread or destiny more closely. Likewise, if you are doing your life's work but you are so busy doing it that you neglect yourself, family, and friends and forgo having fun, you may want to spend time learning how to put yourself in your day.

It is possible to have it all, and this book is intended to help you craft your life in such a way that you are being, doing, and having what you want in your life without it being at the expense or loss of something else. I believe most of you have had fleeting glimpses of this feeling but have been unable to sustain it over any length of time. If you are already living in your sweet spot, this doesn't mean that you will have arrived and no longer have issues or problems. Life, and you, would be pretty boring without some dynamic tension. Dealing with this tension in your way and in your style with no apologies is what your sweet spot is about.

Living a balanced life always revolves around the big three: body, mind, and spirit. In writing *Living in the Sweet Spot*, I address all three; however, I feel like we have always had them in the wrong order. It is my belief and experience that by the time we manifest something in our bodies and minds, we have been ignoring the messages from our spirits, or our higher selves, for a very long time. For example, I have had many people who knew they were in a job they hated but remained in it just because they felt like they had to. Getting a new job might cross their minds daily, but they ignore it with any handy excuse. Eventually the stress and dissatisfaction with the job starts to make them grumpy, which then effects their relationships. They begin to hold tension and stress in their bodies, which inevitably affects their health, and onward the downward spiral goes. As they continue to ignore the messages from their spirit, their body may become more painful and their mind will tend to get depressed, grumpy, angry, or any other joyless emotion, which in turn leads to, at the very least, a fairly unhappy existence. So in this book we will approach balance from spirit, mind, and body with the hope that if you can hear and follow the pleadings of your soul, you can prevent the resistance from taking residence in your mind and body.

How many of us have had the belief that if we just lost that extra weight, we know we would feel better about ourselves and look incredible, which, of course, would lead to the relationship of our dreams? Likewise, if we just made more money, lived in a certain neighborhood, or had a different car then we'd really have it all. If only it worked that way! This book is designed to help you to stop the endless cycle of falling short of creating what you want in your life by looking outside yourself and blaming others. It will help you see where you can take responsibility for making things different and create a better life for yourself.

One critical component to the success of moving our life in the direction we want is to take responsibility for learning to control what we think. Our minds control a good bit of our thought processes, which in turn gives rise to the direction that our lives go. Our minds often operate somewhat unconsciously, and there is a bit of mischief that goes on under the surface. Until we are intentional and consciously direct the ways in which we want our thoughts to go, we are at the mercy of our unconscious mind. Throughout the book, you will be presented with many tools to move you into a place of curiosity, or what I like to call the "Isn't it interesting?" mindset. That is to say, if you can learn to approach any new discovery of yourself with curiosity instead of judgment, you will open yourself to a world of options instead of your limiting beliefs. This helps you to not only understand the mischief of your mind but also to do so without judgment. Judging what we uncover or know about ourselves sends us right back into the loop of not good enough, bad, wrong, or less than. When you are in the loop, you stay stuck in an endless cycle of doing the same thing.

In *Living in Your Sweet Spot*, we explore the neurology of how our brains develop in the way that they do and how this sets up a positive or negative image of ourselves. This will give you a further understanding of the marriage between spirituality and science, helping you to clarify how important the balance of spirit, mind, and body is to the success of living your dreams. The good news is no matter what you discover about yourself, you can change it.

Each chapter could be a book all by itself, and this book is by no means meant to be a comprehensive or extensive analysis of each concept. This book is designed to expose you to a number of thought-provoking concepts that will help you take a good hard look at what is and isn't working for you. Once you have identified a particular area of concern or interest, you may want to explore further with different books, workshops, or teachers. There are questions to answer, exercises and experiences to perform, and, in general, much to consider to get you living in your sweet spot. *Living in Your Sweet Spot* gives you the tools to create the peace and joy within you by living a balanced life no matter where you are in your life journey or what your external circumstances are.

Use this book as a gateway, companion, or guide to help you navigate through what holds you back. Each of us inherently knows who we are at our core. It is just a matter of getting a few layers out of the way and stepping into the person that we always knew we were.

There is only one you on this planet, and you are the only one that is qualified for the job. Your contributions are uniquely yours, and when you are not yourself, the world misses out on your contribution. Think about what the world would be like if Steve Jobs or Bill Gates didn't live their lives authentically. Take a minute and think of how their authenticity changed the way we live and how different it may have been if they hadn't. You don't have to change the world for your uniqueness to matter. Just being you makes a difference. All the lives we touch and the things we say or do each day make a difference.

It is not possible for us to live fully in our sweet spots without living as our authentic selves. The book is intended to challenge the concepts and beliefs that have kept you from living as your authentic self and to bring you home to the person you are.

Throughout the book you will encounter countless heartwarming stories of the struggles, the highs and lows of the journey, and the eventual triumphs from people in all walks of life and every stage of existence—people who are all moving toward their authentic selves and living in the sweet spot of their lives.

In essence, this book is designed to help you bring yourself home to the person you always knew you were. It is my hope that in the end—after reading, considering, and shifting some of the rigid belief systems that have held you back—you will be thrilled to say, "It's good to be me."

I. SPIRIT

LEARNING TO LISTEN
TO WHERE YOU'RE BEING LED

Chapter I

Following the Thread

I t was about twenty-five years ago when the journey began that would change the landscape of my life forever. While vacationing with a group of friends in Park City, Utah, for an annual ski trip, we encountered a "white-out day" with massive snowstorms. Being fair weather skiers, we opted for a day of shopping and going to the spa instead of braving the elements.

We began the day with brunch in one of those places where you wait such a ridiculously long time for eggs that it should be written up in *Food & Wine* magazine. Despite the hour wait, time passed quickly. It helped that the restaurant was attached to a "new age bookstore" so we could walk around while we waited.

We were milling about, wasting time, browsing, and half-heartedly shopping, when a woman began to set up a table to offer card and palm readings. Twenty dollars bought you a fifteen-minute reading and a glimpse into your future. From a distance, my friend observed me as I was watching the woman set up the table. She caught my eye and with her impish grin said, "Dare ya." At the time, still one to be provoked by a challenge, I thought, "What the heck? If nothing else it will make for a great story."

So I went...first. It seems my bravery was all that was necessary for each of my friends to be curious about their own fate. Later, as we sat around the table laughing and joking about our predictions, I chimed in, "Well it seems as though I'm going to have a child! It says so right here"—gesturing to the line on the base side of my fifth digit on the right hand.

My group exploded with laughter. This statement appeared to be the best one that they had heard yet. I must admit that I had laughed too, but inside I was thinking, *It's not THAT funny*. There was a feeling churning inside and just beginning to reveal itself.

I had considered being a mother and decided against it. I already had a very busy life, a large practice to manage and maintain and; I had travelled extensively and had no partner at the time. However, as the cajoling continued, I felt an uncomfortable unease in my being that I couldn't quite put my finger on. It was the inauguration of my beginning to understand what I now know and refer to as "following the thread." Following my thread took me to places I hadn't yet or couldn't have imagined. Following your thread is developing an awareness of the choices that you make daily that bring you closer to living the life that you want to live. When your choice is incongruent with what you want, there is a feeling that goes with it that you either pay attention to or dismiss out of discomfort with facing the truth.

Think about the endless options that you have every day. Everything from whether to have a cup of coffee in the morning to knowing what you want to be when you grow up. These choices shape our lives and define who we are. We are in a constant dance with the universe as we are presented with clues that help guide us. Learning how to listen and respond to these whisperings brings us closer to living the life we were meant to live. It is only by understanding and realizing the pleadings of our souls that we achieve genuine comfort living in our own skin. If we allow our lives to be controlled by what we believe we "should do," we smother the light within us and concede to a life of mediocrity.

It's helpful to think of threads as choices. When faced with a decision to make, our bodies respond on many levels whether we are conscious of it or not. Being able to pay attention and work in harmony with what your body is telling you brings you closer to manifesting your soul's desires. You have probably had the sensation of knowing when something was in line with your desires because it simply felt right. You may not be sure why, but you have the feeling that it's right. Likewise, when you have that gut feeling that something isn't quite right, but you still ignore, dismiss, or deny it, you still deep down know it wasn't right. Often this leads to wasting time trying to convince yourself that it was a good decision when you know it wasn't. There are many threads running through your life at once collectively creating the tapestry that is you. Following the thread is being conscious to the emotional and physical cues (such as pain, fatigue, illness, etc.) and following them through until you understand the gifts they bring.

Each of us has our favorite M.O., or mischief, that we use for justification. Some of us just flat out deny we feel that way. Some of us will enlist others to support us in believing we have made the right decision. Still others will spend countless hours talking and rehashing why they made the decision, still knowing deep down that it wasn't the best choice. Allowing yourself to be led without judging the path or choices you make not only brings you an understanding of how to create your soul's desire, but also reveals the mischief you employ to keep yourself from attaining what you want. Learning to follow this thread means becoming conscious of what you are feeling and then following it through until you understand the reason you were affected. When ignored, you miss the precious gift the situation has brought to you.

It is only curiosity without judgment that enables you to stay in touch with the thread of your life. Self-judgment not only keeps you stuck in the same place but also negates the opportunities you created for yourself. One of the things that I try teach both in my workshops and with patients is that if you can start by wondering instead of judging and come from a place of curiosity instead of judgment, you will gain an understanding of what your resistance is. One of the best ways to do this is to start with the question "Isn't it interesting?" Isn't it interesting that I am so angry, sad, fearful, etc. And then ask, "I wonder why?" Learning to come from a place of curiosity and not judging yourself for having whatever emotional response you have had will give you considerable insight into your heart and soul's desire.

As I think back to the palm reading in Utah, my thread was leading me to a desire that is closest to my heart and one of my soul's greatest desires that was apparently sitting quietly in the background of my consciousness. This was not something I could have predicted nor expected and, if I wasn't paying attention to the thread, it may have passed me by completely. Fortunately, it positively changed my life forever.

Fast-forward a few years later and I found myself thinking back to the palm reading again as my brother and sister started their families. I loved being Aunt Pat and having the opportunity to be in their children's lives, watch them grow, teach them a few things, have a slight influence, and then give them back to their parents. Still, each time I was with them, when I left, I felt something emotionally bubbling that I couldn't quite put my finger on. It was an almost unperceivable presence tapping gently at my attention, hanging in the background yet causing no real perceptible discomfort. It was just an awareness, which I promptly dismissed. I was grateful to have a pseudo-parenting experience without having to take time out of my practice, travel, and social life.

My best friends had been in relationship for about three years when they decided they wanted to adopt a child from China. I was thrilled for them. They are incredible people, and I knew they would be fabulous parents, which they are. I was also thrilled for me. Now I would have the opportunity to have a child in my life, much closer in proximity. What was even more exciting was all the talk about "the village" participating in the raising of this child.

I remember how excited we all were when the first picture arrived. She was a chubby, healthy Chinese cherub with a beautiful smile. I observed each of us as we stared at the picture of this cherub, knowing all of our lives would change forever. Changed in ways that we couldn't even begin to imagine. If nothing else, it was bound to change the way that we would spend time with each other. She was and still is an extraordinary child, and we have all have participated, each in our own ways, to her growth. To this day being a part of her village continues to be an incredible experience.

Two years later, my friends decided to do it again. This time proved to be a very different experience. Their second child had a difficult entry. When she arrived, she was essentially bald, having had her head shaved due to lice. She was quiet and quite fearful and would let very few people hold her. She was fussy, difficult to soothe, and very much within herself. When she began to speak, she had significant speech issues and was challenging to understand. She was easily frustrated and often irritated. In a word, it appeared as if she was developmentally delayed.

Needless to say, we were all concerned. It was significant for me that I was one of the privileged few that she would allow to hold and soothe her. I had no idea at the time what an extraordinary gift this child was giving me, or the profound effect she would soon have on my life. She was worming her way into my heart, and I didn't even know it.

Fast forward to Mother's Day of my forty-second year. I was celebrating the day with friends and their young children. The girls had handmade their precious gifts for their moms as they had year after year, but this year, as I watched them celebrate, something subtle began to churn inside me. It was the kind of feeling that you get when you are irritable, seemingly for no reason, but that stays with you, invading your peace and demanding attention.

I could not identify what I was feeling except to say that as the day went on, I was becoming increasingly, soulfully sad. Intense sadness is a foreign feeling for me so it was definitely getting my attention. Initially, I wondered if I was missing the connection to my own mother that I always wanted but had never quite developed. It seemed like a thread was trying to weave its way into my life, and even though I could feel something trying to make its presence known, I still didn't have any clarity about exactly what that thing was.

Having exhausted the mother issue over the years, I gave it a quick consideration and dismissed it as clearly not the offending irritant. This was a strange and unfamiliar feeling that was gnawing at me. I couldn't put my finger on it and hoped I would soon understand it or, perhaps, it would simply slip away. Of course, neither happened. This feeling was demanding my attention and stayed with me for days until I finally began to uncover the "gifts" this irritant was bringing.

Whenever I get stuck with something I'm feeling and can't figure it out, I try to imagine all the possibilities, no matter how serious or silly they may seem. It is also helpful to remember what was happening and where I was at the time the feeling began. In this case, I went back to the recent Mother's Day experience and began assessing all possibilities.

Did I need to address some issue around my own mother? Was I sad for so many unloved or parentless children in the world? Or was I feeling some grief for my good friend who had just lost her mother? After exhausting a whole host of options, I asked myself the one question I was ignoring: Could it be possible that this profound sadness was because I was not a mother myself?

I hadn't seen that coming. I got that uncomfortable sickening feeling that sometimes happens when you know you are getting the right answer, but it's definitely not the answer you'd thought it would be. I had convinced myself for years that I loved my life, and all its freedom, the way it was. The thing that I hadn't paid attention to was the fact that I had to keep convincing myself.

I struggled for a long time with the possibility of being a mother, wanting to be absolutely sure that it would be a good thing to adopt a little one into my world, especially as a single woman. By now, I was pretty sure it was the right thing for me, but I had to consider what would be best for the child as well. Was it fair to adopt into my world? Would a child be better served with a traditional family that had a mother, a father, and maybe brothers and sisters? Was it right to take a child out of her native land and bring her to America?

In retrospect, these questions seem silly because I know that we were destined to be a family and, were literally, custom-made for each other. I can't imagine my life now without my daughter. The process of adopting, however, demanded trust as I followed this thread. I had to pay attention to every clue, body indication, and emotion that came into my awareness.

All of my senses were on high alert, and awareness at this level isn't always smooth or clear cut. I struggled with this monumental decision and needed confirmation. So I prayed and meditated. When I prayed,

I would ask for a clear and concrete answer . This was too important for anything less than a clear, real, concrete sign to confirm such a huge decision. I wanted an answer that would let me know beyond a doubt that this was the best thing for both of us. I sent my request to the heavens and let it go.

Two months later, I was at an auction at the High Museum in Atlanta. It was a high-end auction that had fabulous prizes for the very few ticket holders that were lucky enough to win. Prizes consisted of things such as guided trips, spa vacations, plane tickets, etc. I considered it more of a donation than a raffle since the chances of winning were slim to none, but it was a good cause.

After paying my respects to the people I knew, I needed to get going and started down the hall of the museum. When I was halfway down the corridor, I ran into a good friend and spent some time catching up. In the middle of our conversation, I heard my name over the loud speakers. The drawings were being done for the auction, and lo and behold, my name was called.

I hurried back into the room and onto the stage where I was handed a large manila envelope. I thanked them, stepped off the stage, went back out into the hallway, and sat on a bench, eager to see what kind of vacation I was going on.

As I opened the envelope, I could see that it didn't look like a travel certificate but more like a picture. I was disappointed at first, but then, as I pulled the image out, I almost fainted. The picture was a beautiful watercolor by a Chinese artist and sealed with his red signature chalk block. The picture was a stork in flight! Tears flooded my eyes, and I felt a hundred emotions at once. I was stunned and knew this was the answer I had been waiting for. I knew, without a doubt, that the universe, God, or whatever you call it, supported my decision and I was going to be a mom. I had my answer. I keep the picture hanging in a prominent place as a constant reminder that all the help I need is out there. I just need to ask for it, know it will come, and wait for it.

Now the real work began. I sent my application to the agency that I had selected and began the process to become an adoptive parent. In a few weeks, they sent me a large package that was to become my dossier.

It turns out that adopting is not for the lazy or faint of heart. An adoption dossier consists of seventeen documents in all. Included are requests for a host of information: tax records for three years; letters of recommendations from three individuals, one of whom must be a family member; a physical examination with all the findings; FBI clearance; local police clearance; a picture book you create, which includes labeled pictures of you, your house, family, pets, and neighborhood; an essay on why you are adopting; fingerprints; and more.

An average couple will take about three to six months to gather all the information required, depending on how much energy they are willing to expend while they manage the rest of their lives. I received my package on a Thursday or Friday and actually didn't even open it because I knew what it was.

Monday evening I got a call from the agency informing me that China had changed the rules on adoption and that they were only allowing a small percentage of singles to adopt per year. The rules were to go into effect that Friday. The reality of this was that one baby per agency per year would go to a single person. She gently informed me that there were others ahead of me in the process and it would be a long time until I was able to adopt from China. She then asked if I had considered any other country to adopt from.

My mind was racing in a hundred directions, and I could feel my heart beating in my throat. I knew in my soul that my child was coming home from China. I had dreamed about it, and the universe had sent me so many confirmations. How could this be? Was I actually hearing this correctly? Was it possible the universe would lead me this far and drop me after I had faced so much? Was it even remotely possible that I was following the wrong thread?

Dead silence.

I don't think I spoke for two minutes while my brain was processing at the speed of light. Then I said, "Well, it's not Friday yet."

She responded, "I know you must be upset, but with all due respect, you have just received your dossier package, and it's impossible to gather all that information in the few days you have. I will call you next Monday after you've had a few days to think about it, and we can talk about what's next. I am so very sorry about this."

I hung up the phone in a daze of utter disbelief. I was feeling lost and didn't know in which direction to turn. Baths have always been a source of comfort and inspiration for me, so I poured myself a glass of wine, got in the tub, and burst into tears. After a gut-wrenching sob, my mind started to calm down, and I began to mull on the possibilities.

As I lay in the tub, I just couldn't understand how this had happened. I had followed the thread. I had listened to the pleadings of my soul. The universe had brought me messages of confirmation. What was this about? Was it some sort of test?

I had been doing affirmations about being a good mom and asking for guidance to be led to know what her needs would be and to provide for them. In an instant, I knew I had to end the pity party, get up, and get busy. I had a dossier to prepare. As unbelievable as it was, I trusted that I would have the paperwork in by Friday. I don't know if it was naivety or believing in miracles, but I knew one thing for sure: I needed to get out of the tub and get on with it. Time was so very limited.

I pulled out the packet and looked at the long checklist to see what, if anything, I could do that night. The picture book was the first thing that caught my attention. I started taking pictures of my dog, my house, and what would be her bedroom. I set up the camera on the piano on a timer and ran back to the chair with a smile until the flash went off.

I printed them and went to the twenty-four-hour drugstore, bought colored construction paper, cut it into sections, and pasted all the pictures with captions and descriptions underneath. Book done. Check.

While I was on the way to the drugstore, I called my friends and asked for the required letters of recommendation, which they agreed to do immediately. I called my accountant and told her what was happening, and she had the personal and business tax records for the last three years couriered the next day. Before bed, I wrote the paper on why I wanted to adopt and sent it to a friend to proofread, and I made a list of what had to be done the next day.

Fortunately, I had already done the fingerprinting and the home study, which takes a fairly long time. I went to work the next day, and just before starting with patients, I called the state to find out how I could get local police clearance and again explained the situation. I'm not sure if an angel answered the phone or what, but she said, "I know I probably shouldn't do this, but go see Mable at the Doraville police station and I will let her know you are coming. I'm pretty sure she will be able to give it to you today." I had no doubt that because I was choosing to be a willing and active participant, paying attention to every detail, and following my thread, this angel was put in my path.

Lunchtime came and I jumped in the car and flew up to Doraville. When I arrived, there was Mable, waiting for me so she could go to lunch. I filled out the obligatory forms and, in about a half hour, I walked out with the documents.

The next hurdle was a letter of recommendation from a family member, and since I had not yet told my mom or anyone in my family that I was adopting, this was probably going to come somewhat as a surprise. Whenever I am working on something that is important and personal, I am fairly private, as I was when I adopted my daughter. I wanted to make sure it would happen, and I wanted to avoid anyone else's opinion influencing me. This doesn't mean that you have to face an issue alone, but focusing in this way helps to clarify what it is that you truly want and feel instead of valuing and placing someone else's opinion ahead of your own. My closest friends, who I knew would help me process what I was feeling without trying to force their own opinions, were tremendously supportive.

I had rehearsed several scenarios in my mind for telling my mom, but rehearsal was over. While I was on the way to the doctor to get my physical, I called her and casually said, "How would you like another grandkid?"

"What? Who? Is Lisa having another baby?"

"No, Mom. Me."

"WHAT! How could that be?!"

"Seriously, Mom, I am adopting a baby from China."

She was thrilled and wanted to hear every detail. I told her I would share the whole story later but that now I needed her to do me a favor and write the letter of recommendation and that it had to be here in Atlanta by tomorrow. I explained to her that she needed to write the letter and FedEx it today so I would get it in the morning. She agreed. Family recommendation letter? Check.

I had called my doctor that morning and explained my situation. She graciously had me come at lunch, and she performed the physical, sent the blood work to the lab, where it was processed STAT and would be back in the morning. It was a hectic first day, but I seemed to be making headway—and believing I could get it done was becoming a reality.

I then called the bookkeeper in my office, who fortunately was also a notary, to explain what was happening and what I needed. She graciously agreed to notarize the documents the next day when I, hopefully, would have them all together. An additional step in the notary process was that the notary had to be authenticated to prove that she was indeed a notary. Gratefully, she took care of getting this document done. Check.

Step by step, the dossier was taking shape. I was getting more and more confident that I was going to make it. The next day I sent one of my staff to get the physical report after the blood work was in. Despite feeling like a train wreck at the moment, I was deemed fit and healthy.

The FedEx from my mother arrived, and the letters of recommendation were hand-delivered by my friends. Taxes were in. Picture book made. Paper on why I wanted to adopt done. Fingerprints and home study added. On Thursday night, as I did the final count, checking off each document and sorting through all of the requirements, I almost couldn't believe it—I had all seventeen documents!

One final hurdle needed to be tackled. All seventeen documents had to receive a state seal. A state seal is a blue piece of paper that has the state seal embedded on it which overlays each document, verifying the document to be accurate and true. "Just keep following the thread, Pat," I'd tell myself.

The next morning before I started seeing patients, I called the capitol to begin the process of acquiring the state seals for each document. As I patiently explained my situation to each person, they passed me on to someone else who they believed was the one who could help me. After being passed through six people, I started in again on my story, and the "gentleman" on the other end of the line gruffly responded with, "Can't help ya," and promptly hung up the phone.

In no way was I going to be deterred by one man having a bad day or by this challenge to my commitment to follow the thread, so I dialed in again. This time an angel answered the phone and told me exactly what I needed to do. I explained to her that I had hired a runner who would bring the documents. She took the runner's name and informed me that when she arrived at the capitol, she should come directly to her and she would personally see that it was taken care of. As she was telling me this, tears of relief welled in my eyes. I was going to make it.

Linda, whom I had hired to take the documents down to the capitol, arrived at nine at my office. I explained whom she should see, and off she went with documents and the gates to the next phase of my life.

The hours went by slowly. Fortunately, I had patients to focus on and was distracted. I can't say that it hadn't crossed my mind about every fifteen or twenty minutes. I couldn't help but wonder what was happening and if it was getting done. It was essential that she return before noon so that I could get the documents on their way to beat the deadline—and the clock was ticking. "Trust the process, Pat. Just keep showing up and following the thread."

At 11:45, she walked in the door, and as I came out of the treatment room with a patient, I looked at her anxiously. She smiled, lifted the documents, and said, "Done." I thought I was going to faint. I had one patient left to care for, and then I would be off to mail the package.

I finished with the patient, scooped up the documents, and rushed out the door. I ran into the FedEx store and waited in line. When it was finally my turn, I walked up to the counter, slid the seventeen documents across, and said to the woman receiving them, "I need these documents to go to this address in the fastest, safest way possible."

She smiled at me, reached across the counter, took both of my hands, looked me in the eye, and said, "I have adopted three. I will take good care of them." I will never forget the tide of emotion burgeoning through me in that moment. I could hardly keep it together.

The state seals make the documents very distinguishable, and anyone who has adopted a child would recognize them right away. I felt as if I was in a time warp and all I could mutter was, "Thank you. Thank you so much."

I paid for the transaction, got back in my car, and sat there for a long silent moment. Uncontrolled tears came flooding out, rolling down my face, part emotional and part relief, as the reality hit me that I had done it. My daughter was in the hands of the universe now and somewhere in the distant future on her way home.

I had followed all of my emotional and body cues, and it seemed as though I was in the homestretch, fulfilling one of my soul's deepest desires, but unbeknownst to me, there were a few more obstacles to hurdle before I would be called "Mom."

About a year later, I received the picture of my daughter. The next step was to write back and confirm that I would accept this angel. Six weeks later, I received the travel plans, which are the documents that permit me to come, along with the details of exact date and time. According to the documents, I would be going to China in three weeks to pick up this child who had already taught me so much.

The following week, a disease called SARS was making its way into the headlines. Severe Acute Respiratory Syndrome was a virus infecting people around the world, and its epicenter was in the Guangdong province of China, where my daughter was born.

I have been diagnosed with asthma, and for the most part, it is a non-issue except during those rare moments when I get a respiratory infection. This disease was highly contagious, and many people were becoming infected and dying daily. It was scary and I really didn't know what to do about it. It didn't help that everybody had an opinion on what I should or should not do.

Should I go now or wait until the epidemic had passed? What if this jeopardized receiving the child whose picture I had now stared at so long it was etched in my soul? I was trying to pay attention to what the fear was telling me, but at times it would engulf me. I was overwhelmed and not sure what to do.

I went home one night after work, sat down, and took a couple of deep breaths. I needed some clarity and needed to remove myself from all the drama so I could hear my body. Soon I felt a calm come over me, and I knew that going to pick up my daughter was the right thing to do. I knew that nothing bad was going to happen. It has always amazed me how much fear can cloud your judgment, and this was no exception. There was no way I was coming this far to be stopped by a disease I didn't have.

My heart and spirit were weary, and my dream was being challenged at every turn, but underneath I felt a calm, trusting everything would work out. I just didn't know how. If permitted, there was no way that I wouldn't make the journey, with or without my friend. I was too close now and had been through too much to get to this point and not go.

Fortunately, permission was granted, and I was finally going to China. After a few tense days, my dear friend decided she would go with me despite the pressure she was receiving from her friends and family. I am and will always be forever grateful to her for coming with me. She remains to this day almost like a second mom to my daughter. She provided extraordinary support and helped get me through the transition from single woman to single mom. I was willing to go alone but so incredibly grateful she was making the journey with me. I would be a brand-new mom with relatively no experience, and she was the consummate, experienced mom with two children. I breathed a sigh of relief. It was all working out.

We arrived in China a few days later, and the following day, we proceeded with our group to a government building where we were to receive our children. When my daughter entered the room, she started doing the beauty queen wave with a huge smile on her face as if she was in a parade, waving to everyone in the room. It was an incredible, magical moment when they brought her to me and placed her in my arms. It's a funny thing having that feeling when you know in a moment that your life will never be the same.

After the adoption, we all went back to the hotel, and my friend, my new daughter, and I set out to do some exploring in China. After a long, exhausting day, we returned to the hotel and each went to settle down in our rooms. As I shut the door of my hotel room, I turned around and saw that little one sitting on the bed, looking at me with her big eyes and smile. I just stared at her and thought of all the miracles that had taken place, all the messages sent, all the threads weaved, and there she was. Finally.

The first night was a tough one though. She cried and cried. And cried. The fact that she was missing her caregivers gave me relief that she was able to emotionally and physically attach to a parent. Attachment disorder is not uncommon in children who have not had a parent present from the beginning. It is a condition that keeps children from forming healthy relationships or being able to bond with anyone. Having attached once meant there was a really good chance she would do it again, and fortunately, she is very attached not only to me, but to many wonderful people in her life.

Morning came and I was awakened by a little hand that had reached through the side of the crib and was stroking my arm. I opened my eyes, and there she was, looking back at me, happy and smiling, and she has been that way ever since. Seems we were beginning to bond and had become a family.

What started as a joke that touched something in me ended with the fulfillment of a destiny that I didn't know I had. Almost unperceivable at first, the thread weaved its way in. Even though I had no idea where I was being led, I somewhat blindly kept following the thread from my family to my friend's family to a museum and, eventually, ended up in China. Prior to following my thread, you never could have convinced me that I would end up being a mother. However, here I am with my soul at peace, being a mom and gratefully loving every minute.

As you read this book and go through the various sections, I ask you to pay attention to the reactions that you have, whether they be emotional, physical, or neutral. Some information you may find helpful, some may irritate you, and some may challenge you to become a better you. I encourage you to allow your mind to consider what are some of the threads that have been running through your life. Have you been present to them or pushing them into the background?

Whatever reaction you have will be nothing more than information. What you do with that information is what really matters. Will you find yourself focusing on what you do well or ignoring what needs to change? Will you dismiss some information with the belief that it doesn't pertain to you, or will you be willing to challenge yourself to find your sweet spot?

Noticing all your subtle or not so subtle reactions will lead you to become more fully conscious about what your sweet spot is and whether or not you are living in it. My goal, as you read this book, is to help guide and empower you to be purposeful and mindful as you follow your own thread and weave your incredible life to fulfill your soul's desires.

Chapter 2

Finding Your Destiny

It's never too late to be what you might have been
–Mary Ann Evans

From a very early age, most begin to wonder, "What do I want to be when I grow up?" This inquiry is continually reinforced by well-meaning adults who ask this throughout our childhood. My mother asked me that very same question one day when I was about four, and I told her that I didn't know for sure, but I knew I was here on a mission. A response that you can be certain I was chided about for years. Well, the truth is that I am on a mission, and it is a mission that I have come to know as my destiny.

So often when we hear the word destiny, it conjures up some important contribution to the planet, like discovering cold-water fusion or writing a symphony, but the truth is that your destiny may be that you are the person who lights up a room with their smile. Your destiny may be that you are the go-to person who can always be relied on for integrity and telling the truth, or you may be the person who develops the sticky notes for 3M. What is important to understand is that each person's destiny is valuable no matter how large or small it may seem in its contribution to the planet.

The Merriam-Webster dictionary defines destiny as a predetermined course of events. It is a concept based on the fact that there is a fixed natural order to the cosmos. This is where Webster and I have to differ. I don't believe that it is a fixed order, and we are not at the mercy of any predetermined outcome. Although destiny and fate are often used interchangeably, it is important to note that they have distinct connotations. Fate is the power or agency that predetermines the course of events, whereas destiny is the finality of events as they have worked themselves out.

Why is this distinction important? Because fate is what you are handed, but you are the person who determines your destiny by choosing what to do with what fate handed you. Each choice you make to follow your thread or ignore the pleadings of your soul will determine the direction your life will take and what will inevitably be your destiny. Sometimes it takes tremendous courage and sometimes just a simple choice, but knowing that you are the one who is making the choice puts you totally in charge of what your life looks like when you are living your destiny.

When I was in my midtwenties, I had a job as a head athletic trainer for a high school, and I was a full-time teacher in an inner-city school in New Jersey. I had no debt, owned my car, and, between both jobs, was making about seventy thousand dollars a year, including a parking space and an assistant. At the time, I thought I was living the high life, and in reality, I was.

As fate would have it, one of my team physicians was a chiropractor, and the other, an orthopedist. At the time, I had no real exposure to chiropractic, and I didn't have any real feelings about it one way or the other. The chiropractor and I got to be friendly and eventually would share our respective rehabilitation techniques. He taught me what adjusting the joint could do, and I would educate him on taping and rehabilitation techniques.

As time went on, I observed that the athletes who were getting adjusted seemed to get better faster and realized that there might just be something to this chiropractic stuff. I say this not in any way to minimize the orthopedists. If I break a bone or need surgery for a meniscal tear, both of which I have had, I go to the orthopedist. However, for many of the injuries that were occurring on the field, it was fascinating to watch the chiropractor reduce subluxations by putting bones back in place and then balancing the muscles to facilitate healing. With no clearly defined objective or agenda, I began to think about going to chiropractic school.

As many of us do when we are thinking about something, we solicit the opinions of others. So I, in my naïve enthusiasm, decided I would go home and tell my parents I was thinking about going back to school. I said to my father, "I'm thinking I am going to be a chiropractor," and he responded, in what he believed to be his supportive way with, "Are you nuts?"

This took me by surprise because my father had back issues on and off for years and always went to the local chiropractor whenever he injured himself. He would get medication for the pain from his physician and then, as he would say, "go get it fixed" by the chiropractor.

"You're making a damn good living, Patti. Don't blow it. Put it out of your mind," he said. So I began to doubt the rumblings brewing in my soul. Should I really consider changing my career? It was going to be another four years in school. I'd be giving up my great salary and going into debt. Maybe he was right, I thought. Maybe I should just be happy with what I have and not rock the boat. Besides, I really didn't know if I had it in me to get through all that and then start a practice. It was risky. Maybe I should leave well enough alone, I told myself.

Destiny had a way of continuing to make its presence known. No matter how much I tried to push it to the background or convince myself that letting it go was best, its nagging presence would surface and recede on regular intervals throughout the next few months. The most pervasive feeling I had was that each day a little piece of me felt like it was dying because I knew I was limiting myself due to my own fear and doubt. I know that if you have ever had this feeling, you can relate to how it silently smothers your dreams as defeat and hopelessness rush in to fill the void. Fortunately, since most decisions aren't permanent, a new course can be set with intention and a change of mind. Add a dose of passion, and you are sure to be on your way to success.

Such was the case for me. I could no longer hold myself back and allow for this inevitable slow death of self. I knew I had to at least try, or I wouldn't be able to live with myself. Making the decision alone began to shift things inside of me, and a new surge of confidence began to replace the fear and doubt that had pervaded my being. I felt like me again. A little scared, but me. I took the first step and began to look at different schools and their individual requirements. It turns out that despite the four years I already had, I still needed six credits of biochemistry to meet the requirements for admission to the school I had chosen. So I enrolled at the college in the town where I was living and took the summer intensity program and ate, slept, and dreamed biochemistry, finishing the course work in eight weeks.

Next, I decided I would place an application with the school and see what happened. I knew I was just delaying the inevitable decision one way or the other, but a little extra time is always good. As fate would have it, I was accepted and was now faced with the choice to either upend my cushy life and follow the pleadings of my soul or remain in my comfortable, predictable, safe surroundings.

Obviously, I made the choice, finished my degree, and have been in practice for thirty years now. Throughout this time, I have continued to learn new techniques and develop new interests, all of which move me closer to the next phase of my destiny, because destiny is not a fixed place in time. We are constantly learning, expanding, and changing. Currently, in addition to my practice, I am hired for speaking engagements, lead workshops, and write. I know these are all part of my destiny because I am at peace with what I am doing. I don't feel like I am missing out on something or that there is something I should be doing. I also have no regrets for not doing something that I wanted to do because I am actively engaged in the things that bring me joy. It doesn't mean I am finished, it just means I'm on the right track.

This is one of the ways that we can ascertain how closely aligned we are with our destiny. There is a certain amount of dynamic tension that is needed to create the passions that drive us onward, but at our core, there is peace. For example, when I was trying to put the thought of returning to school behind me, I felt a low-grade irritability, but as soon as I made the choice to just entertain the idea, I immediately felt relieved. It didn't mean I wasn't nervous, but I knew I had made the right decision because I had a certain amount of internal peace. If you have thoughts of "I wish I had" or "I should have when I had the chance," there is bound to be unrest somewhere within you. This unrest is the dynamic tension that is speaking to you—urging you to take another look. Will you listen to your soul or continue making excuses why you couldn't possible do this or that? The choice will continue to be there every moment of every day.

That's one of the best parts about being human. We are the only species that can literally remake ourselves with a decision at breakfast. We get to decide every day what we believe about ourselves and if we believe in ourselves. If we make a mistake, we can literally change our minds and decide something else by dinner. That's the good news and the bad news. The choice is always yours.

We all dream as children. We want to be firemen, doctors, actors, policemen, dancers, professional athletes, and more. What happens to those dreams? Does the proverbial reality set in? Are we forced to put those dreams aside to honor the restrictions that we believe the universe has handed us or are we handing ourselves those restrictions to hold ourselves back? What about the dreamers who realize their dreams despite multitudes of obstacles in front of them, some far greater than any of our own? Were they just lucky or willing? Even more importantly, how willing are you to dream again? Will you allow those passions to rise? Allowing this passion to drive you closer to yourself may be the bravest thing you ever do in this life.

Living in your sweet spot often involves risk. One risk is that you may be the most content and happy person you could ever imagine possible. You may also be challenged, frustrated, angry, and sad along the way to getting there. We often look at successful people and forget all of the hard work, disappointment, and setbacks that they endured on their way to their destinies.

Consider the great film director Ang Lee. After earning his master of fine arts degree, he spent six years as a stay-at-home husband while his film career stalled. Ashamed of his failure, he briefly considered a career in computer science. His wife urged him to continue to follow his dreams and he of course went on to direct such acclaimed films as *Life of PI*, *Crouching Tiger Hidden Dragon*, *Brokeback Mountain*, *The Hulk*, and many more. He has won two Oscars and several Golden Globes and BAFTA awards.

Or there is Walt Disney. At twenty-four, Walt Disney had Oswaldo the Rabbit stolen from him by Universal Studios. At twenty-five, MGM told him no one would ever like Mickey Mouse because a giant mouse on the screen would terrify women. He formed his first animation studio in Kansas City and, due to nonpayment from a distribution company in New York, was forced to dissolve his company. At one point, he was unable to pay his rent and survived on dog food. Later, when he attempted to get financing for the famed Disneyworld, located on swampland in Orlando, Florida, he was labeled a fool and almost went bankrupt while partially supporting the endeavor with his own money. Today, Walt Disney's animation and motion picture studios and theme parks have developed into a multibillion-dollar television, motion picture, vacation destination, and media corporation empire that still carries his name. Additionally, in his lifetime, he won twenty-two Academy Awards and four honorary Academy Awards, as well as seven Emmy Awards.

Finally, who could forget the successful rise of the British novelist J. K. Rowling? By the end of her twenties, she was a divorced, unemployed single parent on welfare, but she still had her dreams. After being rejected by eight publishers, *Harry Potter and the Philosopher's Stone* was published just before her thirty-second birthday. She went on to become one of the richest women in England with the Harry Potter books becoming the best-selling book series in history. The ensuing films based on the books became the highest grossing film series in history.

I can almost hear what you are thinking. Those are all famous people. They all have talents and abilities that I don't have. The truth is most of them had the same fears and insecurities that we all have. The difference is what you do with them.

My father taught me this lesson without saying a word. He never progressed further than the ninth grade with his education, yet he went on to become a very successful, wealthy businessman. He owned several hotels, restaurants, and bars and was a great man to work for. He told me, "If you have to tell someone who and what you are, then you are not." What he meant by that was who you are speaks for itself. He also said, "That's the good news because it's all in your hands and you are betting on yourself. You have to like those odds." There was no arguing with this truth. He was living it. He was unwilling to make excuses for not living up to his own potential and dreams. Despite having more valid excuses to avoid his dreams than most reading this book, he chose not to. We all have our stories, and the tighter we cling to them the more we allow them to speak for us and define who we are instead of deciding for ourselves. What reasons do you use to hold yourself back from what you want?

One of the ways some stay stuck and never realize their destiny is by telling themselves, or letting society tell them, something frequently enough that they come to believe it—whether or not that thing is grounded in truth. Often a good argument can be made for why it could be true, which is what makes it so convenient to use as an excuse. What do you tell yourself that keeps you from exploring how you might change a situation that isn't working for you or that makes you unhappy? Do you feel like there are no other jobs or situations that are available to you? Are you telling yourself that you should just be happy that you have a job at all—let alone, one that you love? Does it feel like you will have wasted your time and an education if you change your mind? Is someone's approval about your choices more important than your happiness?

I had a patient who worked for a government agency. She told me every time she went to a job site she felt irritable, tired, and annoyed. "Besides all that, my neck is killing me, and I can't turn it in any direction without pain!" she said. She explained that she had been onsite for three months and hadn't been taking care of herself at all. She had been working long hours, and it left no time for self-care. "I hate feeling like this because these people really need my help and they didn't do anything to make me feel this way, but I feel like I take it out on them," she said. "I just get so frustrated and irritable and feel trapped in this job."

Clearly her body was talking to her and telling her it was time for a change. When I suggested this, she told me she had thought about that but dismissed it, believing that no one would hire her at sixty-three and felt lucky that she had a good job. Despite the fact that this woman was one of the best in her field, she still felt like she couldn't do anything else. I suggested that clearly she had an amazing skill set and maybe she just wasn't thinking outside the box.

"I've been in the box so long all I can see are the corners," she laughed.

Part of the way that I work is to help people interpret what their body is saying besides "I'm in pain." Learning to listen to these clues allows us to heal holistically by healing the whole of you, not just the part. Paying attention to your body can also offer clues when you are not in line with your destiny. Each part of our body relates to different aspects of our lives. For example, the throat is the center for expression and how you put yourself out in the world. When I have a patient who can't turn her head in any direction, I know that there is conflict between the heart and the head. When we have conflict between the heart and the head, the neck becomes the battleground and the place where the emotions get stuck. In addition to correcting the structural issue, she can also deal with the emotional component. Her heart was clearly telling her she wanted out of this job, but her mind was telling her she was too old to be considering anything else and was lucky to have a job at all.

"What would you like to do if you didn't have all those theoretical obstacles in your way?" I asked.

She related that she felt she would still have to go wherever the work was, but if she had her choice, she would love to go to Europe for work. She has family there and would love to be closer to them.

She told me that she really did enjoy being of service. It was just that the job she was in no longer felt like service but more like bureaucratic paper shuffling. "I am pretty good at it though," she added.

I explained the heart/head controversy as I worked on her neck. Then I asked her to consider talking with her family to find out what the job market was like in Belgium and what might be possible and maybe just peek outside the box a little. I also asked her to consider making a list of what she wanted in a job without thinking about the limitations.

"You have certainly given me some things to think about," she said as she walked out the door.

A week later, she returned for a follow-up with her neck. She was feeling good and no longer had any neck pain, and she was a bundle of energy. "I hate to rush you," she said with a mischievous smile, "but I have a plane to catch. I have a job interview in Amsterdam. Long story, but the short of it is that I did start poking around at jobs and called my family, and they had heard of a job in Amsterdam at the consulate that I would be perfect for. One thing led to another, and I am going for it."

"I don't know. I think you're too old," I said with a smile.

Just like the woman before, we are generally the biggest obstacle that gets in our way. Many of us have so many preconceived notions about who we think we are, should, ought to, or have to be that living our own destiny isn't even considered. She got the job and is now living in Amsterdam, enjoying her new job and being closer to her family.

Then there is Jamie, who came from a family of a long line of lawyers. Her father and mother were lawyers, as well as her grandfather, uncle, two brothers, and her brother's wife, whom she adored. Ever since she was a child, her life seemed to revolve around trials, whether they were being prepared for, discussed, or tried in court. It wasn't that she minded it really—it was all she knew. Her father owned one of the largest firms in town and was a well-respected trial attorney.

When it came time for college, Jamie was free to choose any profession she wanted. Throughout the years, whenever anyone asked her what her plans were, she always responded the same way with, "I don't know yet." Many were quick to offer advice about what an opportunity it would be to work in the family business. She always shrugged it off and dismissed it as a means of making conversation. Her family supported her decisions, and she was free to study anything she wanted.

When the time came to go to college, Jamie hadn't thought about what she really wanted to study because she was never taught how to say "I want." She decided to take the easy route and go to law school. It seemed like a no-brainer. She would make a great living, not have to worry about finding a job, and knew how pleased her parents would be.

Being able to say "I want" is critical to living your destiny. Early in our childhoods, some of us are given the message that asking for what we want is selfish and bad. Some of these messages come wrapped in statements such as "It isn't always about what you want. Life does not revolve around you" or "Why don't you think about what he/she/I or they want for a change?" Any of these sound familiar? We were not taught this with malicious intent. We were taught this because they were taught the same thing. These early childhood messages are the seeds for how we begin to construct our lives. If we are taught that what we want isn't important, then we begin to look outside ourselves for confirmation about what we should be doing instead of looking within.

No one would argue that thinking and doing for others is not important. Equally important, however, is being able to assess what it is that our hearts desire. It is what shapes our destiny, helps us decide where we will live, what we do for a living, who or if we will marry, how many children we may or may not want, or even something as basic as how we eat.

There are many reasons people have difficulty asking for what they want. For some, asking for what they want means drawing too much attention to themselves, and it is not worth the exposure. For others, the fear of rejection keeps them from saying, "I want." Then there are those who feel they will be obligated to follow through if they say "I want," and they don't want to be obligated or beholden for their choice. Some don't believe themselves the least bit worthy to have what they want. Last, but not least, is the group that prefers that you already know what they want and expect it to come without asking. When it doesn't materialize, there is often some overt or covert punishment that accompanies this lack because you should have known what they wanted and gotten it for them. Being able to live your own destiny is integrally related to being able to do what you want. Think about how limiting it is if you are not free to say things such as I want to study that or I want to go to this country. Take a moment right now and ask yourself, "How free am I to say I want?"

When you are blindly moving in a direction without any real consideration of whether or not it is your heart's desire, you will not only end up doing something you don't want, but find you have disdain for it once you get there. Jamie was one who was on such a path: She heads off to law school and indeed becomes a successful, highly sought-after lawyer. She is constantly getting praise from her clients, family, and friends, and her dad always beams when he is talking about her. There is only one problem: she hates it.

She didn't always hate it. It evolved over time. She noticed it first as irritability, mostly about having to go to work. She also noticed she no longer had any passion about the work that she was doing. She was far too professional to not do her work well, but she was tired of it and more grumpy than she was happy.

She started taking art classes to learn to paint as a stress relief. She delighted in it and found she really looked forward to the classes she was taking twice a week. Eventually she set up a studio in her house and was spending more and more of her free time painting. She had fallen in love with painting, and not only did it relieve her stress, it freed her spirit. Between work and painting, she had very little time for anything else. She started to take one day a week just for painting and then began selling her work at local art shows. Then her work found its way into galleries and art shows across the country.

She was starting to feel stressed from the painting as it became more and more difficult to balance her life as a lawyer with trying to be a painter. Something had to give. What she wanted to do was quit her job as a lawyer and paint full-time but felt she could never do that. After all, she had spent so much time and money becoming a lawyer, she was making good money, and she just knew her parents would be disappointed as well as thinking she was crazy. Her father was already making comments about the one day a week she was taking off. Her paintings were, however, bringing in a good bit of money and it was tempting.

It took many years, a lot of soul searching, and tremendous courage, but she was finally able to leave the law and has become an incredibly successful artist. She is happier than she has ever been. Jamie was like many people who believe that once they have invested time, energy, and money in a specific degree, they are stuck with it, and this prevents them from making changes. Jamie was also comfortable with the law because she was surrounded by it from childhood. Just like

Jamie, people often choose their destiny out of comfort, not because they truly want to be doing it. Certainly, Jamie, like so many, initially made her decision because it also pleased her parents. Consider how any of these situations may be related to how you are living your life and whether you feel it lines up with your destiny.

Then there is Janette. Janette is one of the most diversely talented people that I know. She has a degree in chemistry, an MBA, plays classical guitar, and sings with multiple choirs. Her photography has sold, she works with wood well enough to have made a boat, and is an expert at web design. Janette had so many interests that she couldn't decide what to do, so she didn't do anything. With all that talent and ability, she was constantly struggling financially and had a good bit of shame about it.

One day, while she was lamenting that she didn't know what she wanted to be when she grew up (she was forty-one), I asked her if she would be willing to experiment with it. "What have I got to lose?" she said.

I asked her to make an extremely detailed list of what she wanted in a job—everything including what she wanted to wear, how far to drive, if she wanted to work with or without a team, be inside or out, and every detail she could think of. The two requirements were that she could not put a specific identity on it, and there could be no limitations due to geography, training, or whatever other excuse she could make up. Then she was to begin looking for a job that met those qualifications.

The key components to her wish list included working with a team, working outside if possible, the option to use her design ability, and wearing whatever she wanted.

She sets off in search of her perfect job, and at the end of the day, she has found a job that meets her key requirements. This multitalented, brilliant woman took a job as a landscape person who mowed grass and planted flowers for a major office park development.

The first week she was there it was clear to the supervisor that she was more on the ball than she let on. In the first few days, she made planting suggestions that not only made the beds look more beautiful but saved money and time. Did I mention she was a master gardener?

Two weeks later, the head management from New York had flown in for a meeting. As they drove through the property, they couldn't help but notice how beautiful everything looked. They asked if they had hired a new maintenance company. The manager said, no, they just hired this new woman in grounds and she really seemed to know what she's doing. Thinking quietly, the leader responded, "Why don't you send her up here so I can congratulate her myself."

Later, after putting in a full day, Janette headed up to the office wearing her sweaty clothes and work boots to receive praise from the big boss. He congratulated her and asked how long she had being doing this, and she said two weeks. She explained how it all started with the list that I had her make and she ended up here despite her talents and abilities.

He listened thoughtfully and surprised her by asking her to send a résumé, which she promptly did. The very next week, he called her in for an interview and offered her the job of being the property manager for the very office park she had been planting flowers for. She eagerly took the offer and began work immediately.

As time went on, she noticed that the communication between the parent company and all the other companies was totally inefficient.

Taking a risk, she called the big boss who had hired her and said, "I was wondering if you are aware that we are extremely limited in knowing what is happening at our other companies, and it would be more efficient if I were to create a platform for intercompany communication. I just discovered that our company in Baltimore created a similar product to the one we just did, and it seems like a huge waste of time that could have been avoided if we were able to share information." He said, "Beautiful! Go ahead and create it."

"I am going to need a little help with my current duties if you want me to create it. I can't do both." He sent her an assistant so she could spend more time on this project, and in about six months, it was up and running. She used her web-based knowledge and created an internal communication system that was very advanced and efficient, and everyone was happy with it.

Reflecting on the success of this new project, she thought, "I could make a business of this and do this on my own!" As time had gone on, her confidence had grown and her shame diminished. Despite having to face some fears, she did go on and create her own highly successful company and now designs custom products for companies based on their specific needs. The best part is that she didn't have to sacrifice any of the things that she wanted. She still works with a team, wears what she wants, and is able to work wherever she wants. All of this started with her being able to say, "I want."

What excuses do you use not to go for your dreams? To help you get clearer on your own destiny, consider making a list of what passionately excites you and see if it lines up with what you are doing. If not, begin to explore how you can make that more of a reality in your life. Additionally, when someone says something or you are exposed to something that interests you, explore it because it may be offering you clues to what you want to do. That doesn't mean that everything that excites you is part of your destiny, but everything that gets your attention is worth exploring. Making a list of your dream life with no restrictions, as Janette did, is also a great way to begin to see whether or not you are living your own destiny. You may just create the life of your dreams and be living your destiny.

II. MIND

HOW IT WORKS AND MAKING IT WORK FOR YOU

Chapter 3

Stress, Change, and the Brain

Living in your sweet spot as your authentic self may require you to make a few changes. What you may not know is that the amount of stress you have can physiologically impact your ability to make those changes. There is no dispute that stress plays a role in how well we enjoy our lives. Almost everyone has some degree of stress. What distinguishes how much of a factor stress plays in your life is your ability to adapt to or handle the stressor.

The exact same stressor can produce an entirely different response from one person to the next. Getting stuck in traffic and being late to work, for some, may evoke feelings of shame, anger, road rage, and blame, whereas for another, they may see it as the universe saving them from some unknown calamity and respond by relaxing and enjoying the extra time.

The adrenal glands are two small glands that sit on top of the kidneys, and, aside from assisting in a host of organic responses, help to deal with stress by releasing epinephrine and norepinephrine.

Epinephrine and norepinephrine are two separate but related hormones that are released when you respond to stress. Think of them as the fight-or-flight hormone that gets released when you decide to either stay and deal with the stress in front of you or run from it. It is often discussed in relation to having to deal with a tiger. You either fight it or run from it. Obviously, we are not running from many tigers these days, but the daily stress that we deal with is every bit our current-day tiger. We will discuss this in more detail later in chapter twelve when we explore sleep, but one thing not included in that chapter is the effect the adrenal glands have on your ability to make changes in your life. As you progress through this chapter you will understand why chemicals—such as cortisol—which are released in response to your stress, can make it very difficult to make any lasting changes because of the effect they have on our brains. In order to fully understand how this works, we need to discuss a little bit of brain anatomy and its function.

This is a basic introduction to brain function and is designed to give you a rudimentary understanding of how stress affects your brain and how it influences your ability to make changes. It is important to understand what is actually happening when you are under stress and how that directly influences whether or not you will be able to make the changes that you want. The significance of stress and its effect on the body and brain is often neglected because it's not something that we can see. By making you aware of these effects, it is my goal that you at least have cause for pause when experiencing stressful situations and understand that you have more control than you realize.

To understand how the brain is affected by stress, we have to look deep within the center part of the brain—inside the limbic system. Think of the limbic system as our emotional center. It is considered the primitive part of our brain and contains the amygdala, hippocampus, hypothalamus, and the cingulate gyrus. It's the part of our brain that controls emotion and motivations specifically as it relates to survival. The limbic system is responsible for how we emotionally respond to the events that occur in our lives and determines which memories we store and, more importantly, the significance we assign them.

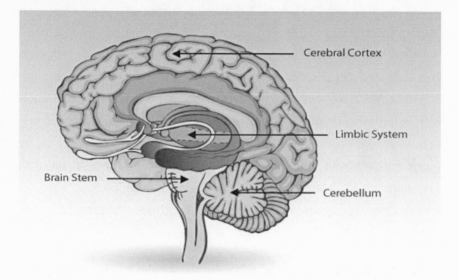

The limbic system also affects how we respond by influencing other systems such as the autonomic, nervous, and endocrine systems. For example, if we see an aggressive dog that is off leash and a dog has bitten us in the past, the amygdala is stimulated and responds by sending warning signals to all parts of our body. Our heart and breath rates increase signaling us to be ready to respond quickly to go into flight or fight mode to protect ourselves. This is accompanied with memories flooding our consciousness of—the last time we encountered the same or similar situation. Even if you have an encounter with a sweet and loving dog, initially, you will have a similar response/ feeling that you had with the aggressive dog. It is only after we begin to use higher cortical function that we can discern incoming information and assign a different meaning to it. In essence, as in the case of the dogs mentioned above, this means that you stop responding from the stressed place, calm down, and recognize that it is not the same aggressive-dog experience that you had in the past.

In the following example, you will see how Lola's consistent exposure to the stress in her home life led her limbic system to respond conditionally, which took quite some time to change even with consistent change in her environment. Lola is a very bright, articulate fourteen-year-old girl who came from a very difficult family situation in which she and her siblings were consistently exposed to an environment of verbal abuse and neglect. She was frequently threatened with being kicked out of the house if she didn't respond appropriately to whatever demands her mother placed on her. Lola was exceptionally smart and while in tenth grade, through a series of events, had the fortunate opportunity to live with another family, attend a better school, and experience many more life situations. She jumped at the chance.

The family she was placed with was the exact opposite of her own family experience. It wasn't as if they were June and Ward Cleaver with Wally and the Beaver but they spoke to each other with respect, love, and seemingly truly cared for one another. There was never any yelling or verbal or physical abuse. They would ask her how her day was or what homework she was working on and genuinely cared and were interested in what she was doing. Prior to this, no one had ever asked Lola how her day was or what she was thinking, and if they did show any interest at all it would be used against her in some way. This new behavior was foreign to her and difficult to trust. All of the siblings treated her as if she were part of the family and included her in everything—asking her to football games, inviting her out with friends, or to the movies. For Lola, it felt magical. However, she found it very difficult to trust this, despite the fact that they were genuinely very loving and inclusive in the way they treated her.

Despite this loving environment, after years of living in her previous environment, Lola was reluctant to trust this new way of life and found she was constantly waiting for the honeymoon to end. She couldn't believe or trust that people could be so consistently nice to one another. Even when they had disagreements with one another, they dealt with it and it passed as if nothing had happened. There were no long-lasting grudges or hurt feelings. She remained on guard, believing it was only a matter of time before they would disagree about something, and she would once again have to leave and return to her previous life—if they'd even let her come back. Her amygdala was conditioned for survival and her adrenal glands kept her consistently on alert.

Think of the amygdala as the alarm system for your body. It is primarily about survival. When stimulated we respond by going into flight or fight mode, which signals the adrenal glands to release epinephrine or adrenaline. For example, if you are constantly under a microscope at work and you have one of those bosses that can't be pleased and is always criticizing your work every time you have to deal with him or her, your body automatically releases hormones that prepare you for whatever is coming. Even if it they are just nodding hello to you, your body will begin to release these hormones because you have been conditioned to respond to this stress. When we experience persistent stress and continually release epinephrine, the cortisol levels raise in our bodies. Cortisol is a glucocorticoid steroid hormone that is released when you are exercising, responding to stress, waking up, and doing many other daily functions. Cortisol causes glycogen to be released for energy as well as a host of other responses, which will be detailed throughout this chapter. When the cortisol levels get too high, they can cause many damaging effects to our physical and emotional well-being. These high levels affect your sleep, disrupt your hormonal system, lower your sex drive, and affect your fat distribution, just to name a few.

It is important here to distinguish that when we refer to stress and its effects on the amygdala, it isn't just the dramatic events, such as the house alarm going off, that trigger this response. More significantly, it is the day-in-day-out, pedal-to-the-metal, stressful way that many people live. When the amygdala is continually stimulated, most of our emotion and motivation are related primarily to self-defense.

This is significant because high cortisol levels prevent new patterns from developing in the brain by affecting the hippocampus—the moderator of the amygdala and the cognitive mapmaker. When you are learning something new, the nervous system sends the information to the amygdala, which changes the neural pattern. This occurs by laying down new neurological patterns. What that means is that when you are under constant stress and producing high cortisol levels, trying to make any kind of change becomes extremely difficult from a neurological perspective. When the amygdala is consistently activated, you remain in a hyperactive responsive state. Neurologically, your brain stays in a reactive state as opposed to a proactive state. You stay in a state of readiness, preparing to handle whatever issue comes your way, and continually release adrenaline and cortisol. When you are in this state, there is very little opportunity for creating, dreaming, or changing. You stay in a state of readiness for survival, and creating remains low on the hierarchal-needs ladder.

You may have heard the statement: "What wires together fires together." What this means is that with repetitive behavior, the neurological bond becomes stronger by recruiting more neurons. Over time as more neurons are recruited to produce the same behavioral response, the response gets quicker and is more easily triggered. Each one of our cells is programed to respond to whatever neurological message is sent, and the whole body in turn responds accordingly. For example, if you are someone who has a tendency toward depression, when you experience it, the neurological patterns that you have established over time send a chemical message to every cell, which responds according to its specific innervation. When you want to change these deeply rooted neurological patterns, you must give your cells new messages. In doing so, you begin to lay down new neurological tracks in your brain that move you away from your conditioned response of depression and to consider other ways to respond to the same situation.

The renowned brain researcher Robert M. Sapolsky has shown that sustained stress can damage the hippocampus and, therefore, new learning and memory. The high cortisol levels remain much longer than the adrenaline and continue to affect brain cells even after the immediate stress is diminished.

The problem is that high cortisol levels cause shrinking and inhibition of the hippocampus. When the hippocampus function is diminished, the amygdala is left unregulated, which in turn keeps you stuck in survival mode, and when you are in survival mode, your cortisol levels rise. What that means in simple terms is that as your cortisol levels rise, they turn down the hippocampal response so no change occurs. This is why it is so imperative to find ways that work for you to decrease stress on a daily basis, and in the coming chapters, we will discuss many ways to do that.

In Lola's case, it wasn't until she was able to trust her new environment that she was able to stop excreting adrenaline and reduce the cortisol levels. She was then able to make new associations in her brain, make different choices, and create new memories. Think about how this may relate to your own life. Have you ever been involved in a bad relationship or job and found yourself waiting for the same thing to occur in your new relationship or job? Think about how you have felt when you get up to go to work and face the same bad boss who doesn't appreciate your work or believe you can do any better. Has it left you with the feeling of *what's the use?* Do you have the feeling that you're stuck and that your situation will never change, so you might as well accept it?

Part of our difficulty in making changes has to do with how our brains develop from birth on. As we develop, our brain progressively uses faster brain waves, and consequently, our cognitive function becomes more discriminatory. When we are very young, from the ages of birth to two years of age, we use only delta brain waves, which are the lowest brain wave levels. Delta brain waves measure from .5 to four cycles per second, and as adults, these are the brain waves that we utilize when we are in a deep sleep. As infants, we view the world just as it is. There is no assessing, filtering, or editing, just information coming in.

Somewhere between the ages of two and five or six we begin to utilize the theta waves, which measure from four to eight cycles per second. It is in this wave range that the child begins to have a low level of discernment and much more of a tendency to live in an imaginary world. In this stage, we do more recording than any type of critical thinking. This stage is a critical stage in that the messages that we are given are recorded in our subconscious. In fact, from birth to about age six, we are basically just recording machines. Everything we are told or experience, we record in our subconscious.

If a child consistently gets messages that they are less than, not good enough, too fat, too slow, not smart, or ugly, these messages become the rulers of his or her subconscious mind. If these continue or are reinforced into our later years, and the child does not have the drive or capacity to determine what is true and what isn't, these messages become the scaffolding of what the child comes to believe about him or herself.

During ages six through twelve, the alpha brain waves begin to come into play. Alpha brain waves measure between eight and thirteen cycles per second. It is during this phase of development that we begin to try to make sense of the data that is coming in. In this stage, we still have active brain waves of imagination firing and often find it difficult to distinguish fact from fantasy. This is why during this stage, we have an easy time pretending. Think about the games we played as children. We knew we weren't cowboys or Indians but reveling in the fantasy of it came easily.

During this phase, as we continue to receive message of less than or not good enough, they further reinforce the earlier recordings and, little by little, begin to build the framework that we eventually come to believe about ourselves. Think about the message that you continually received in your own life. Some common messages that children receive are: "How could you be so stupid?" "You will never amount to any-thing." "Why can't you be more like..." "Nobody likes a fat kid." "What is wrong with you?" "How stupid are you?" The following story further exemplifies how these subtle and not so subtle messages influence our lives.

From a very early age through to her early adulthood, Nicole's father consistently told her she had a pea-brain. As a young child this was very confusing because, in reality, she was very smart and consist-ently received praise for success in school from peers and teachers. Her father had not finished his education and found Nicole's brightness somewhat threatening, but Nicole didn't know that because he was very successful. In order to maintain control, he consistently minimized her. This sent messages to her unconscious brain that no matter how smart she was or what praise she received there was always the message in the background that she was stupid. Nicole responded by minimizing herself, shunning praise, and diverting focus onto others and away from herself. If someone gave her praise, she was quick to divert it and give the credit to someone else or would say something like, "I couldn't have done it without so and so."

When faced with two different realities, as in Nicole's case, you can respond one of two ways. You can begin to accept the lie as a truth, or you can rebel against it. Initially, she minimized herself, but eventually became rebellious, and "I'll show you I'm not stupid" became the unconscious impetus and drive for much of the success she later created. She continued to enjoy success in every area of her life, which only added to her confusion because her father continued to call her a pea-brain. Remember, as she was aging, her brain waves were developing as well, and she was now able to question her reality. Despite this ability to question, years of being told she had a pea-brain were firmly rooted in her subconscious. Although the rebellious effects were positive in the long run, it wasn't enough to negate the underpinning of this core belief that she had about herself. She continued to think that she needed to prove herself to be successful, to feel lovable.

The last stage of brain-wave development occurs between the ages of eight and twelve and beyond. It is during this phase that theta and gamma brain waves are measured as anything above thirteen cycles per second. At this point, we consciously begin to analyze our thinking. We take information in, discern what is and isn't true, and assign meaning to each piece of data as it relates to our lives.

In her late teens and early twenties, after years and years of being called a pea-brain, Nicole began to wonder why it bothered her so much since it clearly wasn't true. As her success grew, the absurdity of calling Nicole a pea-brain lost its effectiveness, and her father changed tack and began to give her new messages to minimize her self-image such as, "Nobody likes a show-off" or "Don't draw attention to yourself. It's not ladylike." Despite all the success she had academically and in sports, she could never fully allow herself to acknowledge or feel the success.

In her early twenties, Nicole began to explore her feelings about how her father had treated her. It was at that time that she discovered that her father, who was a very successful businessman, had a secret. He had never graduated from the ninth grade. As a result of his insecurity, he had tried to put down his precocious daughter in order to feel better about himself. Having a good support network, Nicole was able to process her feelings and eventually move into compassion for her father, who had clearly felt shame for not being educated.

Although Nicole enjoyed a good bit of success, her story is not that different from most of us. We were all given messages as children, some of which still run our lives today. As children, we either react by trying harder, giving up, getting angry, acting out, or doing anything else that isn't really our authentic selves but our survival selves. It is only when we are able to keep our amygdala out of a reactive place that we can dispel the unconscious beliefs about ourselves that hold us back from the lives we want to live.

Think about what messages you had as a child and what, if any, impact they are having on your life today. Some life events we assign more significance to than others, and depending on where we store them, those same events can have far reaching and triggering effects many years after the initial insult. Such events become filters or lenses that influence the way we see any current event that is similar, and they often become triggers in adult life.

If Nicole had never dealt with her feeling of continually being called stupid, there is a good chance that whenever someone alluded to the fact that she didn't understand something, she would be triggered once again and respond defensively. It's the way our brain responds because that is how it's wired. In order to live as your authentic self, you have to gain an understanding of the unwanted and untrue messages that you have stored since childhood and begin to challenge them.

These defense mechanisms are the methods with which we learned to protect ourselves as children. At the time, our choices were brilliantly masterful because we clearly survived. We may have minimized ourselves, stayed quiet, not drawn attention to ourselves, protected our hearts, or used any number of ways to stay under the radar, but they worked well. However, there comes a time when the mechanism that once protected us holds us back and, as adults, prevents us from creating the very thing that we want. To make changes, there must be an understanding of what defense mechanisms we use. A good therapist, pastor, or spiritual teacher can assist you if you have trouble uncovering your defense mechanisms. Working through your issues can be scary or difficult at times, but the reward is definitely worth the effort.

One thing we can count on is, whether or not we are mindfully making changes, we are all constantly in a state of change. Our bodies age, our environments change, and we consistently understand things in new and different ways, even if we don't want to. Change truly is inevitable. One of my favorite sayings is: "Once you know, you can't not know." What you do with that knowing is up to you, but you can no longer consciously negate what has been learned. For example, once you know that you are allergic to wheat and you know it produces reactions in your body, you can no longer not know the truth. You still have a choice about whether or not you eat the wheat, but you can't deny its effect on you.

There are many reasons that people choose to change what isn't working. Some changes are forced by getting fired from a job, getting a divorce, or having to go to a DUI class, and others because something isn't working and we truly want to do things in order to be different in our lives. When we set out to consciously transform something that no longer serves us, there are two ways in which that change occurs. They are classified as first-order and second-order change.

First-order change is usually doing more or less of something that we are already doing and is reversible. There is also no significant new learning that occurs. For example, assume you want to change your body. You may need to eat more or less, or you may need to work out more or in a different way, but there is essentially no new learning that occurs. You may need to learn different techniques for working out or you may learn a new way of eating, but essentially, nothing is dramatically different. More importantly, you can reverse it. Once you have decided that you no longer want to eat differently or work out in that way, you can revert to your old habits and behaviors. This is not the case with second-order change.

Second-order change is deciding or being forced to decide to do something fundamentally different from the way that you have been operating. Second-order change causes you to see things in an entirely different way. Once you have this new understanding, it is irreversible. Second-order change is very different in that you can no longer revert to understanding or seeing things in the old way again. In the following story, Dobie exemplifies how second-order change can permanently alter our perspective.

Dobie is a thirty-five-year-old woman who believed she was unlovable and that deep within her core something had to be wrong with her. As with many, this belief system stemmed from an early childhood event to which she assigned specific meaning. When she was a little girl, she was extremely frightened by nightmares. As the limbic system was stimulated, her amygdala responded, and as she awakened in terror, she would run to her mother's bedroom, but when she arrived, the door was always shut tight and locked.

Pounding on the door, she would plead with her mother to let her in, but her mother always refused and would speak through the door, telling her she would be all right and to go back to bed. Dobie reluctantly would go back to her room and, after staying awake as long as she could, would eventually cry herself to sleep. Dobie deduced that her mother didn't love her, and Dobie believed she was not worthy to be loved by anyone. She felt that if the people you are supposedly able to count on continually let you down, you couldn't count on anyone to love and support you. She felt that if she did trust someone, it was just a matter of time before she would be disappointed.

It was difficult for Dobie to trust people because of her earlier experiences with her mother, and as an adult, she found it difficult to establish meaningful relationships, especially romantically. Her brain had been conditioned from an early age that people would not be there for her when she needed them, and as a result, she rarely asked for anything from anyone. It wasn't until she met a man that she was totally in love with and with whom she wanted to share a future that she enlisted the help of a good therapist to work through some of these issues that had caused her other relationships to end.

As is often the case, we suppress bad memories and Dobie was no exception. Despite what happened as a child, she maintained a fairly good relationship with her mom. She found it easier after her mother had divorced her father prior to his death because she never really felt close to her father and felt as though he didn't really like her. Throughout the course of her therapy, she made frequent mention of the nightmares and her mother's response to them. Her therapist proposed the possible benefits of having her mother come into a session and shed some light on what was going on for her during that time, which could possibly provide a different perspective. Dobie thought it was a great idea and agreed to talk with her mom about it.

Dobie's mom quickly agreed and was willing to help in any way that she could. During the first session, Dobie was nervous about broaching the subject of what she perceived as her mother abandoning her in her time of need. With some good coaching from her therapist, she began to explain how wounded she was as a child when her mother would not let her in her room and soothe her when she had her nightmares or, seemingly, whenever her father was around.

Dobie's mom listened attentively, and when Dobie had finished, she took a deep breath, sat silently for a moment, and quietly began to tell her side of the story.

"Your father never wanted children," she began. "He was extremely narcissistic and I really didn't know or understand it at the time. I, too, have been working with someone to heal the wounds from that marriage so that I can develop healthy relationships. In order to have children, I made an agreement with him that I would always continue to put him first. Part of that agreement meant that once you were in bed, my sole attention would be to him and only him.

"When you came to the door, he would get extremely angry and threaten to leave or punish you if I even so much as opened the door, and I knew he meant it. He was a sick man and, at the time, I was a very weak and naïve woman. It broke my heart every time you came to the door, and in fact, the depth of the love that I felt for you was the thing that finally helped me to get strong enough to divorce him."

Dobie sat there in stunned silence. After years of believing that her mother didn't care about her and that she was unlovable, she was faced with an entirely different reality. Her mother did love her and that love was what made her mother strong enough to leave her marriage and face her own issues of self-worth and love.

"Why didn't you tell me this before?" she asked her mother.

"Until this moment, I never knew that you believed you weren't loved. In my heart I knew I loved you more than anything in the world. You were young when we divorced, and it would have been inappropriate to tell you any details of the marriage. It wasn't until now that I knew you had this issue. I am so sorry. I had no idea that you felt this way."

Her mother got up and wrapped her arms around her daughter, holding her and reassuring her that she loved Dobie more than anything in the world and asked forgiveness for all the pain that she had caused Dobie to feel. Dobie burst into tears, releasing years of pain and suffering. In that moment, new neurological tracks were being formed in her brain. She was experiencing second-order change. She now had information that refuted all of her old beliefs about why she believed herself unlovable.

Lola, Nicole, and Dobie all faced similar experiences in that, as the stress they experienced caused changes in their brains, they made judgments about themselves that simply weren't true. Each of them had to find a way to decrease the stressors and face the truth. This holds true for each of us. Reducing your stress doesn't always have to mean having some spiritual experience with lighted candles, music, and meditation. It can be as simple as taking a few breaths, counting to ten, taking a walk, or listening to music. What matters is that you become conscious and aware and intentionally manage your stress and reactions and avoid reacting from the unconscious child brain. For example, someone says something that reminds you of a message that you consistently received as a child, such as "How did you miss that?" and you can feel yourself being triggered. Stop in that moment and take a breath or pause to help yourself recognize that the person in front of you isn't the person from your childhood or previous trauma, but someone trying to help you. This is managing your reaction, and with a little bit of awareness and practice, it will stop over time.

When dealing with your day-to-day stress, it is just as important to learn to control how your body is responding. Managing your stress isn't always about being triggered by a childhood message. Controlling your adrenal response and the flood of epinephrine is every bit as important when dealing with stress. Not long ago, I got up in the wee hours of the morning to do some writing that had to be done on a deadline. I was fully engrossed in the process and hadn't been paying attention to the time. My first patient was at eight, and I hadn't showered, let alone figured out what I was going to wear. Needless to say, I was in hyperdrive, and my adrenals were flooding my body with adrenaline.

I dressed, jumped in the car, and sped off to work. I pulled up to a light just as it changed and bemoaned the fact that I had just missed it. It was at that moment that I realized just how out of balance I was. There was no way I wanted to take this energy into the office, and I knew I had to slow down. I put the car in park, closed my eyes, and took ten deep breaths. I opened my eyes and continued to breath as I waited for the light to change.

When I pulled into the parking lot, I took another minute to take several more breaths with my eyes closed. It was a simple measure but it worked well, and I walked into my office ready to be present to the needs of my patients, my staff, and myself. If I had not taken the time to pause, slow down, and control the adrenaline coursing through my body, it would have impacted every aspect of my day.

There are many ways that you can decrease your stress and some may work better for you than others. No matter what methods you employ throughout the day, I recommend that at some point you find an extended time to meditate or be quiet.

Some possible suggestions for decreasing stress are:

• *Step away from the technology!* I can't tell you how many times I have stepped into my waiting room to get the next patient, and every single person is sitting there focused on his or her phone. Emails, texts, and taking care of business actually promotes more stress than it alleviates. I know many of you are right now making the mental argument that when you take care of things it leaves more free time do leisure things, but what most do with more free time is use more technology. Taking a moment to just sit peacefully and listen to music or page through a magazine will have a much greater calming effect than getting things done on your phone. I have friends who are so addicted to their technology that when we travel together, I have to lock it in the hotel safe so we can just focus on having fun. They have confessed that they love it when I do that. Think about the last time you didn't have access to your phone or computer for whatever reason. I know it probably felt disconcerting at first. However, didn't you at some point find yourself just relaxing and surrendering to the fact that you couldn't use them? Consider doing this intentionally when appropriate throughout the weekday or weekend. It may surprise you how much stress your technology is creating.

- *Take a nap.* I'm not a big napper myself, but I do find that if I take ten minutes and set the timer on my phone, close my eyes, and just rest, it shifts my energy into a much more relaxed and calm state.

- *Take a short walk.* I'm not referring to a walk for exercise but a short five or ten minute walk around the block to change how you feel and slow you down. Getting up from your desk and stepping away from your work for a few minutes will make you much more productive in the long run. Movement shifts your excess energy into a much more productive place.

- *Get out in nature.* Sit and watch the birds or the wind blow the trees. There is much evidence advocating being out in nature as a way to bring your stress level down. I find when I take my dog to the dog park (leaving my phone in the car) and sit there watching birds fly and the trees blow while she runs around, the experience chills us both out!

- *Breathing.* Taking ten or more deeps breaths almost always calms your body down. You can simply follow your breath as it flows in through your nose inflating your lungs while your diaphragm expands to fully extend your belly. As you slowly release your breath, feel the softening of your belly and relaxation of your body. Take a moment to honor the pause in between the breath. You can also be more specific and breath in your desired response and breath out whatever is causing your stress. For example, you might focus on breathing in the feeling of relaxing your muscles and, as you breathe out, focus on releasing the stressful project you're working on.

- *Shoot the breeze with your friends or neighbors.* Taking time out to chat with your neighbors on your porch, on the sidewalk, or in your driveway is a great way to relax. I have some patients who have developed the fine art of what they call "porching." This involves neighbors dropping in, sitting on the porch with no agenda, having a beverage, talking, and hanging out.

- *Use your imagination.* Close your eyes and picture yourself in a place that brings you peace. See yourself at the beach, in a meadow, or on top of a mountain. Imagine all that you can about where you are. What can you see? How does it feel? What is the temperature? Focusing on these things will put you in a state of relaxation.

• *Consider reducing stimulants.* Drinking coffee, soda, tea, and fruit juices throughout the day makes it difficult to relax and increases anxiety. Consider drinking herbal tea or lemon water instead.

The more you are aware of your stress, the more you are in charge of your stress. The more in charge you are, the more likely you will be to make the choices and changes that you need to live your authentic life in the sweet spot.

Chapter 4

Meditation—Learning to Turn Down the Noise

Meditation has been around for thousands of years. No one knows exactly how long, but most scholars agree that it has been around for about five thousand years. Think about that for just a minute and ask yourself what else has that kind of staying power. If something has been around that long, doesn't it pique your interest to know why?

Research studies on the benefits of meditation are countless, and with regular practice, meditation has been shown to lower cortisol levels, increase concentration, reduce blood pressure, decrease stress, increase immunity, increase your awareness, and, in general, produce an overall calming effect. In order to live in your sweet spot, it is necessary to have effective tools to bring down the noise levels in your life on a regular basis. Meditation is a simple, effective tool that can be done anywhere and anytime and requires no equipment.

Let's face it. We all have a certain amount of stress in our lives and managing our stress is critical to living well. There is a good chance that most of you reading this book are probably in some way trying to make positive changes in your life, and you are aware that stress has many effects on our body. One effect of stress is that it causes the cortisol levels to rise in your bodies. Cortisol is a glucocorticoid (steroid hormone) that is normally released in response to events such as exercising, acute stressful events, or waking up in the morning. Cortisol in its normal function will cause the release of glycogen for energy, counteract inflammation, and convert protein to energy. When cortisol levels get too high, however, they inhibit your ability to make long-lasting changes in your life, which is discussed in greater detail in the previous chapter on stress and change. Meditation is an excellent way to bring the cortisol levels down and enable you to make the changes you want to occur.

When considering the negative effects that stress has on your body, as well as on the quality of your life, having a tool to reduce or alleviate stress becomes invaluable.

I have had many people tell me that they have tried meditation but simply find it impossible to meditate for more than one or two minutes before they lose their focus. Not all meditation involves sitting in a lotus position with soft music and candles, and with rare exceptions, everyone can find some form of meditation that works for him or her. Below are a number of different techniques for meditation, and I encourage you to explore them all and find one or more that work best for you.

Preparing to Meditate

Some believe that in order to meditate properly, you must create a special place and set aside a specific time to provide the ultimate meditative experience. While finding a tranquil peaceful spot with an abundance of time is optimal, it is not the only way to achieve a powerful meditative experience. In fact, it is often the reason people don't meditate more frequently.

I often use the time in a carpool line, waiting for an appointment, or other small snippets of time to meditate. Taking this time can also have an impact on the quality of the experience that follows. If I have been having a normal busy day then jump in the car to pick up my daughter at school, I find sitting for ten minutes and meditating while I wait totally affects how I am going to interact with her when she comes out and gets in the car. Inevitably, I am more present and relaxed, and I enjoy sharing the time with her when she arrives. In this way, taking the time to meditate significantly helps the transition from one experience to the next.

Ideally creating a space that is free from distraction is optimal. When you are a beginning meditator, I suggest that you find a place that is quiet and will allow you to focus with minimal distractions. Consider your bedroom, a quiet spot in your garden, or even your office if you are able to shut the door and not be disturbed. However, as you become an experienced meditator, you will find that you will be able to tune out the outside world and go into that in-between space of infinite possibilities with relative ease. I've created a beautiful meditation space in my home, but I will be honest and say that I rarely use it. Most mornings, I will sit in the comfy chair in my home office and meditate for twenty or thirty minutes before my house starts to wake up. Doing this helps me start my day calm and focused, which in turn has a positive effect on how I interact with my family, patients, staff, etc.

One thing that I have found consistently with new meditators is that they often give up because they are not good at staying focused immediately. It's important to realize that meditation is a practice, and it takes practice to be more in charge of your mind. Some days you will be better at it than others. The important thing is to do it daily. There are some days that I have incredibly profound meditative experiences and other days when I have trouble focusing for two minutes. It's all about taking the time to do it.

People often ask what is the optimal amount of time to meditate? There is no exact perfect time for meditating, and it also depends on how much time you have. A daily meditation practice may be once or twice a day and may reasonably vary anywhere from fifteen minutes to an hour. If you have the luxury of being on retreat or vacation and time for meditation is limitless, meditate as much as feels comfortable.

Regardless of how much time you have, I recommend that when you do begin, start slowly. People consistently tell me that they sit down to meditate for half an hour and quit after a few attempts due to frustration believing they just can't do it. As a beginning meditator, trying to meditate for half an hour is an unrealistic goal and sets you up for failure. Fifteen minutes is a good starting point, and time can be added from there. Focusing on smaller amounts of time initially will help you achieve a higher success rate.

Thirty minutes a day is a good goal to aim for. Our body rhythm is generally most quiet in the morning and in the evening. Meditating in the morning sets the tone for the day, and evening meditation signals your body to slow down, promoting a deep, peaceful sleep and is also a great way to let go of the stress of the day. Instead of reading to help you go to sleep, try to meditate for a half an hour instead. Often the things that we read before bed will ramp our system up, especially if the book is exciting or suspenseful. Additionally, we often stay up longer than we want to just to finish a chapter. Meditating before bed will signal your body that it is time to relax and slow down.

No matter where you meditate, I highly suggest that you set a timer, especially when your time is limited. Otherwise, thinking about how much time has passed or is left often distracts your attention. This avoids the distraction and allows you to achieve a deeper state of meditation more quickly. I use my iPhone simply out of convenience, but any timer will do. When you set the alert sound, choose some type of soothing melody instead of a harsh disruptive foghorn or piano riff. This prevents you from being jolted out of a relaxed meditative space. When your time is unfettered, I encourage you to forgo the timer and meditate as long as you feel comfortable.

Sitting in an upright position with your feet on the floor and hands comfortably in your lap is generally a good meditative position and promotes alertness while being relaxed. Don't worry about palms up or down; just be comfortable. Avoid trying to meditate lying down because the likelihood that you will fall asleep is high. Having said that, if you are sick and spend a good bit of time in bed, lying down is just fine.

One type of meditation does not fit all. Some meditation practices are designed for relaxation, and some are designed to induce altered states of consciousness. I encourage you to explore some of the following options, especially if you are new to meditation. You may find some more appealing and have greater success with one type over another. Additionally, one type of meditation over another may be more appropriate based on the time you have.

Types of Meditation

- *Breath Watching*: As the name suggests this type of meditation is about being aware of your breath during your meditation. Start by being seated in a comfortable position, closing your eyes, and paying attention to your breath as oxygen fills your lungs and then again as it is gently expelled. Counting is a good way to focus your breath while breathing in and out. For example, as you take a breath in, do so to a count of seven. Honor the slight pause in between the inhalation and exhalation. Follow the exhalation with the same count of seven. As you become comfortable with the rhythm and pace of your breath, discontinue the counting as it can be distracting. Once you feel proficient, focusing your attention on the space behind your eyes referred to as your third eye will increase your experience—as you breathe and meditate. For centuries, this space has was believed to be a center for expansion, and awareness and focusing your attention here will enhance your experience.

- Breathing correctly is not only important for mediation, but for everyday life as well. Correct breathing involves slowly bringing the breath in through your nose, which engages your diaphragm, and allowing oxygen to the fill the bottom of your lungs. You want to breathe in such a way that your stomach fills and your belly pooches out slightly. Generally, when people are asked to take a deep breath the first thing that happens is the shoulders, chest, and ribcage rise. In reality, this actually limits the breath. Avoid lifting your shoulders and rib cage as you breath in and focus on filling your belly. When performed correctly, you will feel your stomach gently push out then deflate. As your mind wanders, refocus on the air going in and out of your nose and throughout your body. Practicing whenever you have a few minutes of time such as waiting in a line, at a red light, or for an appointment will have you breathing correctly in no time.

- *Clearing the Mind Meditation*: This meditation requires you to empty all your thoughts from your mind, allowing your mind to rest. When your mind is at rest, a sense of peacefulness takes over. For this meditation, the most optimal situation is to sit in a comfortable position with a relaxed, erect spine, preferably in a quiet place with no distractions. As thoughts begin to enter your mind, you gently release them and focus on being void of thought. You can be certain that thoughts will enter your mind, and this is expected so don't give up because you are not doing it perfectly in the beginning. This meditation takes a good bit of practice because our tendency is to have thoughts continually float to the surface.

• *Body-Focused Meditation*: In this type of meditation, you focus on your body parts. I suggest starting at the base of your feet and working up toward your head. As you focus on each body part, you breathe into them, allow that part to relax, and let go of all tension. For example, begin by focusing on your left foot, and allow it to relax until you feel no tension remaining. Once the left foot is devoid of tension, move to the right foot then work your way up each leg to your waist and continue until you reach the top of your head. As your mind wanders, you gently bring it back to focus on whatever body part you are working on until it is completely relaxed. This type of meditation is also very helpful when you are preparing to perform in any way and need to be relaxed.

• *Walking Meditation*: Walking meditation is meditation in motion. This technique involves focusing on your body and your environment while walking down the street, a hallway, pacing around the house, or taking a run. Try focusing on the wind or sun and how it feels on your body. You could also focus on how light or heavy your body feels as it connects with the earth. As your mind starts to wander, refocus and concentrate on the movement of your body and the rhythm of your breath. Pay particular attention to the feeling of your feet as they touch the ground and your rhythm as you move. Focusing on your breath is especially helpful when you are running, as it is often rhythmic, dynamic, and meditative in and of itself. When you stop, pay attention to how it feels to stop being in motion. What emotions are you having? Are you light and joyful, bored, or introspective? What else are you feeling and what messages are you giving yourself? This meditation can be done anywhere, and I find it particularly helpful when transitioning from one event to another, such as from meeting to meeting or while walking to the car to go somewhere.

• *Mindfulness Meditation*: This is a practice utilized by many Buddhists, known as vipassanna or insight meditation. Mindfulness meditation involves focusing on what is happening around you, while at the same time being aware of your thoughts and feelings as you meditate. The purpose is not to change anything but to observe all that is occurring. When you are deeply conscious of the thoughts that you have, you are significantly more present to what is happening around and to you. Awareness lends itself to choice. Your mind should be open to your true feelings with no judgments. The monks use it as a way of self-awakening. You can start by just watching your breath, noticing the flow of air into your body and then out again. Then move your attention to the thoughts in your mind and the sights and sounds that surround you. You may find yourself beginning to notice the hum of the air conditioner, followed by the birds chirping outside or the noise of the traffic in the distance. The key is not to analyze or judge anything. The purpose is to simply become aware of all that surrounds you. You do not place any value, judgment, or meaning on what you observe, you just observe. One thing that I find particularly helpful with this is that when you observe certain things about yourself while not judging them, you are then able to make changes that you want in your life. You can't change what you don't know.

- *Transcendental Meditation*: Transcendental meditation involves the continuous chanting of a mantra until a pseudo-dreamlike state of mind is attained. It similar to a lucid dream when one is not actually dreaming but, at the same time, is not fully present. This is useful for those who are easily distracted, as chanting a mantra will prevent your mind from wandering. If you are meditating alone, you may use any word or phrase that works for you. You can either repeat it out loud or in your head. In some traditions, an experienced master will choose a word or phrase for you, such as "sharti," which means peace.

- *Zentangles*: Zentangle is a method of creating beautiful images from repetitive patterns. It is fun and relaxing, and almost anyone can do it. It increases focus and creativity and provides artistic satisfaction, along with an increased sense of well-being. One of the things that I like about this technique, especially for the beginning meditator, is that it is not threatening, you can't do it wrong, and drawing/ doodling is something that we have all done at some time. Traditionally, drawings are done in three-and-a-half-inch squares, and the goal is to fill up the entire square with any type of repetitive drawing that you want. Start out with no specific intention, allowing your mind to empty and be focused on the drawing instead of your thoughts. You have probably done this many times in the past without really realizing it. Think about how many times you have done a doodle in very much the same way, letting thoughts wander and then dismissing them as quickly as they come as you started to pay attention to and focus on the shape you want the doodle to take.

This is just a sampling of some of the many types of meditative techniques. If you are limited in your experience with meditation, I encourage you to try a number of these different techniques. Some will appeal to you more than others. Take your time and be patient with yourself. It takes a little while to feel comfortable meditating. It is important to remember that the goal is to calm your mind and enter the gap of space between your conscious and unconscious mind providing a relaxed state. In doing so, you become in charge of your mind instead of your mind wandering on in endless chatter.

What to Expect

You can be sure that your meditation will be interrupted by thoughts. This is normal and having thoughts does not make you an unsuccessful meditator. Remember that you are learning to control your thoughts and this is part of the process. As your thoughts bubble to the surface, simply let them go and return to focusing on your breath, body or mantra.

If you are using a mantra to meditate, it is possible that you may have thoughts while you are repeating the mantra. If this happens, let go of the thought and return your focus back on the mantra.

It's important to have realistic expectations, especially when you begin to meditate. Evita is a seventy-four-year-old woman who came to one of my workshops and had no prior meditative experience. She loved the meditative experience that we shared during the retreat and vowed to make it a daily practice.

I ran into her many months later and asked how the meditation was going. She relayed that she had tried for about a week, but just couldn't get the hang of it and had pretty much quit. When I asked her what she meant, she told me that she would sit every day for about twenty minutes and could only clear her thoughts for about five minutes.

"That's actually really good," I said. "It takes a while to learn to meditate and control your thoughts, and it may take you a year or more to feel like you're really in charge."

"I'm so happy to hear that," she exclaimed. "I really loved meditating but felt like I would never get it right, so I just quit. Knowing it just takes time makes it feel a whole lot more doable."

I also explained that she should not expect a smooth learning curve. Some days you will find it easier than others to meditate. Being stressed, anxious, or overly excited will all have an effect on you when you begin to meditate, and sometimes we are more in control of ourselves than others. Meditation is a practice, and it takes practice to become proficient. Being patient with yourself is essential.

If you aren't already meditating, I encourage you to challenge yourself to set a goal to meditate for twenty-one days straight. This will encourage meditation to become a habit, and with practice, you will find it becomes easier with time.

If you find that you are having difficulty with meditation, I encourage you to find a teacher in your area to work with who can help get you on the road to successful meditating. Make sure you find someone who is experienced and with whom you feel a good connection. Guided meditation is another option whether you are having difficulty meditating or not. A guided meditation is one in which someone guides you on a journey, step-by-step, to a calm, serene, peaceful state. Lastly, going on a meditation retreat for a few days is a good way to get specific instruction and a whole lot of practice in a short period of time.

To live our lives authentically and feel the deliciousness of the sweet spot, there are times that we need to quiet our minds to hear the pleadings of our souls. While meditation is not the only tool for going within, it is extremely effective, and I encourage you to make it a daily habit and look for the magic to unfold in your own life. If nothing else, it has clearly shown to be effective to reduce your stress, decrease cortisol production, and positively impact a whole host of health issues.

Chapter 5

Gratitude

*Don't cry because it's over, smile because it
happened.*
–Dr. Seuss

As I was driving to work one morning, I began thinking about my upcoming fifty-fifth birthday, letting my mind wander with what I wanted to do. I, like most of us, really don't need or want anything, but I always try to do something a little special on the landmark birthdays. While I was thinking of different options, my thoughts drifted to my cousin Larry and his unusual custom of giving to others when it is his birthday. Then the thought occurred to me that it would be great if I could do fifty-five random acts of kindness for my birthday. It seemed totally doable and I had almost three weeks to get it done.

As I started thinking about all the fun things I could do, the thought occurred to me that it would be really wonderful if I could get fifty-five other people to do one act of random kindness. I thought it would be an incredible gift to all the recipients, those doing the acts, and myself. I started asking my friends, the kids, neighbors, and any patient that I thought would be willing to participate, and in a day and a half, I had reached my goal of fifty-five people.

Everyone was incredibly gracious and willing, so I figured why not go big. I set my sights on getting 155 people. The requirements were simple enough. You could do your act before, during, or after my birthday. You could choose to tell me or not. The only requirement was that if you had agreed to do an act of kindness, you did it. Simple enough, right? Gratefully, the number ended up much larger, with hundreds of people participating.

This was, without question, one of the best things that I ever did. The response was incredible, and the things that people did were amazing! The acts of kindness consisted of all kinds of big and little things. Included were such things as:

- A meter maid letting fifty-five people go whose time had run out on the meter;

- Paying someone's gas bill anonymously so their gas wouldn't be turned off;

- Picking up an elderly woman's newspaper during a downpour and putting it at her front door so it wouldn't get wet;

- Carrying groceries into the house and putting them away for the next-door neighbor on crutches;

- Giving a homeless woman twenty dollars without her asking;

- Taking baked goods anonymously to the teachers at her school with a note that read, "For all the hard work you do that is never acknowledged;"

- Paying for fifty-five people behind him at the Route 400 toll booth (the toll booth attendant said she loves when that happens because it is so fun for her to deliver the news and watch the people's faces);

- Multiple driving kindnesses by many people;

- Paying off a ridiculously high vet bill for a pet rescue foundation;

- Giving someone a twenty dollar tip for a five dollar meal and walking out before they could thank them;

- Helping a neighbor get their sick Great Dane in the car and then going with them to the vet's;

- Paying for an ill friend's house to be cleaned;

- And so many, many, many, more that are too numerous to mention.

One of the most interesting side effects was that people told me that after they had done one act of kindness, it felt so good that they intentionally did several more. I smile every time I think about all of the goodness and the positive shift in energy that had to occur. Interestingly, both the receiver and giver were grateful. One received the positive benefits of the gift given and the other, was grateful to have the means and ability to provide the act of kindness.

The Institute of HeartMath is a recognized leader in researching the physiology of emotions, and according to their research, true feelings of gratitude created by acts of kindness and other positive emotions can synchronize brain and heart rhythms, creating a measurable shift called coherence. Instruments that measure heart rate and brain waves simultaneously measure coherence. When a person experiences feelings such as gratitude, their heart rate and brains waves appear in smooth, wavelike patterns that are in sync. Anger, frustration, and other negative emotions create chaotic and disruptive patterns between the heart and head.

Doc Childre, founder of HeartMath, and Dr. Rollin McCraty have outlined the scientific research in their e-book, *The Appreciative Heart:*

the Psychophysiology of Positive Emotions and Optimal Functioning (2002).
Some of the findings include:

- Increase in immunity as measured by levels of IgA antibodies, which are the first line of defense against pathogens in the body.

- Biochemical changes as measure by improved hormonal balance and an increased production of DHEA, which assists in many body functions including antiaging.

- Sustained acts of kindness and appreciation produce an accumulated effect, and coherence becomes easier to achieve. This is because with repetitive acts, the neural pathway gets strengthened and the coherence is more easily attained.

The people who already did acts of kindness on a regular basis commented that the intentionality of doing this act specifically as a gift to me made it more special for them in addition to their fortunate recipients. People called and wrote me to say that they heard what I was doing, and even though I hadn't asked them, they just wanted me to know that they had participated and would then go on to tell me the things that they had done.

It was magical and, more than once, brought me to tears. It has truly been a gift that continues to give. One person said that they had been so moved by the experience that they had decided to take a hundred dollar bill out of the bank each month and give it to someone when they most needed and least expected it. She has related some incredibly funny stories about people's responses when they receive the money. Each time she does it, she does it a little differently. Sometimes she just hands it to them and walks away, and other times, she gets creative.

She and her husband go for long walks every weekend. On one such walk, she went up to a truck that had two workmen in it. She looked at the man sitting behind the wheel and said, "If I gave you a hundred-dollar bill, would you be willing to spend it on someone you love and do something nice for them unexpectedly?"

"Say what now?" the man responded

So she stated it again, and as she was telling him the guidelines, her husband stepped in and said, "Yes, it is for real, and she does this all the time."

The confused man graciously accepted the hundred dollar bill, and they went on their way. What he did with the money we will never know. Whether it went for his own benefit or he did something for his wife, child, or friend, positive energy was created and someone was grateful.

I never anticipated this kind of response. It was an idea that just took off and created a cascade of good feelings for all those involved. I also felt incredible gratitude for the amazing response and willing-ness of everyone to participate and bring about all the kindness that evolved. This magical experience was simply, without question, the best birthday ever. Even though it was really all about doing kindness and creating gratitude for others, it was the best kindness I had ever done for myself. I invite you to consider doing a day or a birthday or a moment of an intentional act of kindness. I believe it may shift you in ways that you haven't yet imagined.

Gratitude can and will change your life. It is as simple as that. Grat-itude as a practice can do more to change your attitude, body chemistry, sleep patterns, and life circumstances than diet or exercise ever will. Many of the people who participated in my birthday experience related that it was the first time they had consciously been aware of how much being able to create an act of kindness for someone else actually brought them as much, if not more, gratitude by being able to create joy in others. It is important to note that it's virtually impossible to live in your sweet spot without some form of gratitude in your life.

Interestingly, the study of gratitude began only as recently as 2000. Historically, gratitude has been the positive focus of the religious side of the fence, while psychology and psychiatry have traditionally focused on the source of distress or negative thinking. Since religions aren't generally in the business of scientific study, the positive effects of gratitude have been assumed at face value.

So what exactly does gratitude mean? Gratitude comes from the Latin word "gratus," which means thankful or pleasing. Gratitude is an emotion expressing appreciation for what one has, as opposed to a consumer oriented emphasis on what one wants or needs.

Although gratitude can have a number of different meanings depending on the context, in general, gratitude is the appreciation of what is valuable and meaningful to oneself; it is a general state of thankfulness and/or appreciation.

Some additional definitions included gratitude as a moral virtue, an attitude, an emotion, a habit, a personality trait, and a coping response (Sansone and Sansone, 2010).

Studies show that not only can you deliberately cultivate gratitude, but it also increases levels of well-being and happiness in those that do. Additionally, grateful thinking—an expression directed towards others—is associated with increased levels of optimism, energy, and empathy.

There have been a number of studies designed to understand the efficacy of gratitude. Robert A. Emmons, of the University of California, Davis, in conjunction with Michael E. McCullough, of the University of Miami, created one such study (Tierney, *New York Times*: November

21, 2011). It was a relatively simple study during which participants were instructed to keep a journal and list five things for which they felt grateful, using a one-line sentence and performing this just once a week. Interestingly, after two months, compared with the control group, the people who kept the gratitude journal were more optimistic and felt happier. They also reported fewer physical problems and spent more time working out.

Watkins and colleagues (Watkins et al., 2003) found that feelings of gratitude were beneficial to subjective emotional well being. Watkins and his colleagues tested a number of participants using different gratitude exercises, which included such things as thinking about a living person they were grateful for, writing a letter to deliver to someone they are grateful to, and writing about someone they were grateful for. The control group was asked to describe their living room.

The results showed that the participants who engaged in the gratitude exercise showed increases in their experiences of positive emotion immediately after the exercise and this effect was strongest for the participants who were asked to think about the person for whom they were grateful. Surprisingly, the people who already had grateful personalities to begin with showed the greatest benefit from the gratitude exercise, and, for the people who are grateful in general, life events have little influence on experienced gratitude (McCullough, Tsang, and Emmons, 2004).

Dr. Brené Brown, a shame and vulnerability research professor at the University of Houston's Graduate School of Social Work, has uncovered an entirely different aspect of gratitude (2012). It seems that gratitude is the antidote for "foreboding joy." You may be wondering how foreboding and joy landed in the same sentence. The research shows that most of us have a hard time experiencing joy because we need to prepare for the disappointment of losing it. It turns out that we actually practice dealing with the loss of joy because sustaining or allowing for joy requires vulnerability, which not many of us have a good handle on.

We don't want to experience the hurt that comes from disappointment, so we literally rehearse the disappointment. That way, should anything happen, we are prepared and not devastated. In reviewing her research, I was personally touched by an example she gave in which she describes a parent standing over their sleeping child and feeling the most incredible heart-opening love they have ever felt, only to be followed by the heart-wrenching feeling of "Oh my God, what if something happens to them?"

I could totally relate to this experience, not only when watching my daughter sleep, but also later when she would go away on a trip with friends. The thought would cross my mind of "What if something happens? What would I do? How could I handle it?" Knowing thoughts are powerful things, I would end up admonishing myself for having the thought. Round and round it went until I began practicing gratitude in earnest.

These different research perspectives each come to a similar conclusion: the experience of gratitude for those around you and your life circumstances offer physical and mental benefits. In my own experience, by shifting my focus back to gratitude for having this incredible child in my life, I create more coherence in my heart rate and brain waves. The more coherence I have between my heart and head, the more joy and positive feelings I create. This overrides my foreboding feeling about whatever tragedy I believe may occur.

Recently, I had a patient who came in to see me for as she puts it, "A tune-up."

"I'm not really having pain anywhere, but I am incredibly irritable and negative and not feeling comfortable in my own skin, and I was hoping that you could help me figure out what's going on in my body," she said. As I worked on her body and asked her a few questions, it seemed to me she had lost sight of what was important, spending too much time and energy on what was making her negative and very little on what fed her emotionally and spiritually.

I said, "I know this may sound simplistic, but when I get in a negative place, I find the best way to recover is having gratitude for the things that I am grateful for. The more negative I am, the simpler I start. For example, if I am really negative, I might start with being grateful for a bed, shoes, toilet paper, actually having a toilet to go the bathroom in, or having running water."

"That must be why I keep looking at the gratitude kit that is on my shelf!" she exclaimed.

"The what?" I asked.

She explained that it was a Christmas gift from eight months prior that teaches you how to be grateful through a number of different exercises. I told her I didn't think that she really needed a kit to be grateful, but it might be helpful to get started. A few days later, she emailed me telling me that "the gratitude thing" had worked, and she had given the kit to someone for whom she was grateful.

I have found one way to generate gratitude is through random acts of kindness. When someone is not expecting anything, and they receive some act of kindness, especially when they don't know where it came from, it generates feelings of goodness and a lift in their energy.

Consider creating gratitude as a practice for yourself. Gratitude is an essential component to living in your sweet spot. I think of it more as a practice than a habit. Just as you would practice the piano or a sport, it is something that gets easier and better and more efficient over time. That way, when you really need it for yourself, it is a well-honed skill that comes with ease and that you can depend on. This is especially true when you really want to stay present with any extreme joy that you are experiencing instead of worrying about losing it.

Some suggestions for your practice are as follows:

- Create a gratitude journal and write five one-line things that you are grateful for. It can be anything at all, simple or involved. The best part of doing this is that it puts you in a better mood for going to bed and you will sleep better.

- Write a letter to someone and tell them how grateful you are for them or how they have changed your life for the better. Not only does it help you, but the other person also gets a glimpse of how much value they may be in the eyes of another person.

- Instead of counting sheep while you are drifting off to sleep, count gratitude as suggested by Robert Emmons of UC, Davis.

- If you have children, when you are tucking them in at night, ask them to tell you one thing that they are grateful for and let them know what you are grateful for. It will teach them the practice, and it is a delightful way to go to bed.

- Post words, photos, or objects of gratitude in your home.

- Pay attention to your thoughts and, when a negative one creeps in, replace it with something that you are grateful for.

- When eating dinner at night instead of or in addition to saying grace, go around the table and have everyone say one thing that they are grateful for.

- Text your loved one some message of gratitude when they least expect it sometime in their day. Something simple, like thanks for making the bed or cleaning the dishes or that sweet kiss before you left, will go a long way to creating not only gratitude, but a sweeter intimacy between the two of you.

With regular practice, gratitude will lift your spirit and those around you and is integral to living in your sweet spot. Aside from all that, it just feels good!

Chapter 6

Forgiveness

*The weak can never forgive. Forgiveness is the
attribute of the strong.*
–Mahatma Gandhi

Stop and think about it for a minute. Is there anyone in your life that you need to forgive? If so, holding on to negative feelings is one of the most destructive things you can do to yourself. That's right, to you. When we are in the position of needing to forgive, it usually means someone has done you wrong. For many of us, holding on to resentment creates a false sense of power in that you're right and they're wrong. The problem is that it isn't actually power at all.

Unwillingness to forgive creates a fortified emotional wall that keeps us from connecting with others and gives a false sense of protection. Unfortunately, it also walls in the negativity, anger, and resentment that we feel from the hurt. The real danger is when we become a slave to resisting forgiveness, and those unwanted feelings creep into all areas of our lives without our even being aware of it.

It turns out that study after study finds that forgiveness has an impact on a whole host of things. Forgiveness reduces blood pressure, heart rate, and depression and opens up avenues of creativity while, at the same time, allowing you to be more vulnerable with yourself and others. "Five for 2005: Five Reason to Forgive," in *Harvard Women's Health Watch*, discussed five positive health effects that had been scientifically studied. These included:

1. *Reduced stress*: Researchers found that mentally nursing a grudge puts your body through the same strains as a major stressful event, causing muscle tension accompanied by increased blood pressure and sweating.

2. *Better heart health*: One study found a link between forgiving someone for a betrayal and improvements in blood pressure and heart rate, with a corresponding decrease in workload for the heart.

3. *Stronger relationships*: A 2004 study showed that women who were able to forgive a spouse and feel benevolent toward him resolved conflicts more effectively.

4. *Reduced pain*: A small study on people with chronic back pain found that those who practiced meditation focusing on converting anger to compassion felt less pain and anxiety than those who received regular care.

5. *Greater happiness*: When you forgive someone, you make yourself, rather than the person who hurt you, responsible for your happiness. Additionally, one survey showed that people who talk about forgiveness, especially during psychotherapy sessions, experience greater improvements than those who don't.

Take Nicholas for example. He is a thirteen-year-old boy who was forced to switch to a different school because his parents were divorcing. He was very angry with both parents, but particularly his father, whom he blamed for the divorce. When he started at the new

By Appointment Only

PAT GIBSON, D.C.

411 W. Ponce De Leon Ave.
Decatur, GA 30030
Telephone: (404) 378-4686

Chiropractor
Author, Speaker

GibsonChiropracticClinic.com
ComprehensiveWellnessForLife.com

school, he felt extremely insecure, and his anger caused him to shut down, making it difficult for him to make new friends. Aside from that, he wanted to punish his parents for the divorce and didn't want to give them the satisfaction of knowing he was making friends. In his naivety, he didn't realize that he was the only one suffering. Fortunately, he had a teacher who recognized his pain, and after developing a connection over time, she was able to convince him to enter a group that was being offered at the school for children dealing with divorce. With reluctance, he entered the group for the first time scared and closed down. Within a few minutes, as he listened to the students, he realized that what he was feeling was the same as the others, and he began to relax knowing he wasn't alone in his pain. Over time, Nicholas was able to express what he was feeling and, with the help of the group, was able to understand how his anger and inability to forgive was only hurting himself. Over the next few months, Nicholas was able to forgive his parents and return to his happy-go-lucky self.

Almost everyone at some point has been deeply hurt by the actions and words of another. It may have been something seemingly unforgivable, such as a partner having an affair, or as simple as a friend lying to you about something insignificant. However, in terms of the drain on your energy, it really doesn't matter how big the hurt was. If you find yourself rehearsing it over and over in your mind, continuing to think about how you should have said this or how dare they, one thing you can be certain is that it is sucking the life out of you.

Despite the many things that you may know about forgiveness, here are a few things you may not know:

- "Forgiveness of self and others has been the most powerful predictor of both depression and suicidal ideations" (Ahadi and Ariapooran, 2009).

- "Over an extended period of time, inability to forgive can be experienced as negative emotions that result in a cascade of biological and brain responses. Findings about the body's hormone response to forgiveness reveal that the inability to forgive is reflected in specific cortisol levels, adrenaline production and cytokine balance (Worthington 2005), with patterns that parallel those reported in people living with high stress. These hormone patterns are known to comprmise the immune system (Berry and Worthington 2001; Seybold et al. 2001) with the long-term consequence of several identified chronic illnesses (Danese et al. 2007)."

- "Chronic unforgiving causes stress. Every time people think of their transgressor, their body responds. Increasing your capacity to forgive cuts down on your health risk. Now, if you can forgive, that can actually strengthen your immune system" Everett Worthington.

- Recent research reports that "a number of chronic health conditions have been identified as health conditions with social and interpersonal etiologies (originations) and consequences. Forgiveness interventions offer important insights for the management and treatment of these conditions" (Elliot 2010).

As you can see, forgiveness or the inability to forgive can have far-reaching and pervasive effects on your health, your relationships, and your ability to create joy in your world. In my research, I have found that there are essentially two steps in the process of forgiveness: grieving and releasing. Grieving is fairly straightforward. It is the time you allow yourself to feel the anger, trauma, hurt, or betrayal, and it is essential to being able to let go in the second step. There is no absolute time frame to this step but it seems that, despite the offense, most people should be finished with their grieving within a two-year period. If not, there is a good chance there is a much deeper wound being dealt with.

Sometimes forgiveness is quick and easy, and sometimes it's a layer at a time. It doesn't matter how you get there, the important thing is that you keep heading in that direction. If it is your intention to forgive, you will, whether it takes a moment, months, or a lifetime. Most people understand that forgiveness as a concept is a great idea, but the trouble is most don't know how to go about it. Many people report that they try repeatedly to let it go in their minds, but nothing changes. Forgiveness is sort of like parenting in that it doesn't come with a manual, but almost all change that occurs comes from the heart, not the head. You cannot undo what has been done, but you can see what has been done in a new light, and this step alone will put you well on your way to forgiveness.

Fred Luskin in his book *Forgive for Good* says the key to forgiveness and letting go of anger and hurt, no matter what the offense, is to be mindful and focus on gratitude and kindness. He also adds that forgiveness concepts are simple. It's the execution that is hard. Forgiveness is freedom for you, not your offender. I believe this to be the most overlooked concept related to forgiveness. Many people believe that somehow forgiving their offender will let them off the hook, pardon them, and condone their actions. This couldn't be further from the truth. The only person that gets let off the hook is you.

Have you ever found yourself holding onto a grudge when the other person isn't even aware that you are upset? They have long moved on, but you find yourself holding on, letting the hurt churn inside. Your pain in no way has any effect on your offender. There is a misconception that by staying present to our hurt we can somehow prevent further wounding. Unfortunately, the only purpose it serves is for us to stay more present to our pain. Whatever they did is something they will have to live with. Letting it go doesn't in anyway diminish the fact it was painful, but holding on to it only continues to give it life. When we fiercely hold the energy of being wronged, which is just another way of staying right, we expend countless hours letting the incident run through our minds, going over it time and time again. The only thing that generally comes from this is that we get to relive the anger over and over. We become caught in a vicious cycle of expending endless energy for an event that has long been over.

Inability to forgive someone allows him or her to get you twice: first, with the initial wounding and, second, when you hand over your time and energy by holding onto the pain. Personally, this alone has been enough for me to let go and forgive as quickly as I am able.

Many years ago, someone had done me wrong by betraying me. In reality, she had betrayed herself more than me, but being a sensitive soul, I was affected deeply. Little by little, I started not trusting people, and I wasn't even aware that it was occurring. It felt like a low-grade pervasive stress that I couldn't quite name. I started wondering in the back of my mind if someone was going to follow through with what he or she said they would do and then brace myself on the chance that they wouldn't. I had never been like that before this, and I really didn't like the feeling but chalked it up to getting older and needing to be more mindful. Periodically, the old hurt would run through my mind, begging to be set free, but no, I held on. I was never going to let myself be fooled like that again!

One morning I was lying in bed, letting my mind wander and review the day. I became aware that I was worried if an upcoming event would happen as planned and worried whether the plane would be on time and wondered if the purchase I had paid extra for early delivery would get there on time. It dawned on me how much of this stress was about trust. When did I get this way?

I never remembered feeling like that before, and I recognized how much irritability I was feeling in that moment. Over the next few weeks, I began to examine this behavior, and as time went on, I was able to trace it back to the betrayal that had occurred. I was creating doubt and not trusting others in my life over what this one person had done. I was the only one suffering. Gratefully, with time, awareness, and intention I was able to get back to trusting fully again, but without the power of forgiveness, it would have never happened and I would have continued to live my life in a certain level of doubt and a low level of irritability.

Forgiving others is only half of the forgiveness equation. Self-forgiveness is the other half. Self-forgiveness is often overlooked and usually more difficult. In general, it is easier to forgive someone else than it is to forgive yourself. We are wired for mastery and can be so hard on ourselves whenever we make a mistake that it is often hard to let it go for fear that we may repeat it again. As a result, our self-judgmental whipping stick is always close at hand.

Forgiveness of self is one of the most positive steps you can take to move forward and create something new. Doing so frees your mind, reduces tension in your body, and allows you to move on to creating new opportunities. The inability to forgive yourself chains you to the past and prevents allowing for the very things that you are trying to create. Forgiving ourselves is often harder than forgiving others because there is a misguided notion that if we forgive ourselves we will some-how let our guard down and, possibly, make the same mistake again. The fear of reliving that pain keeps us from having the very thing that we want.

For some, forgiving themselves is difficult because they are afraid that they will lose their sense of self that has been built as a result of the anger, vulnerability, and resentment that they have accumulated over the years. This is the method they have devised to protect themselves from further harm but, unfortunately, keeps them from embracing life with joy. This is not an authentic self—it is a wounded self. The wounded side of them is more attached to staying protected than to taking risks to get what they want. To live in your sweet spot, you have to create as much distance as you can from your wounded self and step into your authentic self. This does not mean to deny or ignore the wounded self but not to leave it in charge. It's the act of being able to recognize when your fear is present but managing to keep it in the background as you proceed to do whatever you're doing or creating.

Marcia is a very bright, articulate, accomplished fifty-three year old woman who, at an earlier age, was raped by a man she knew. The rapist was violent, and in her inability to escape or prevent the act from happening and for fear of her life, she did not resist him. It is now thirty-three years later and she still has feelings of guilt for not fighting back. Her inability to forgive herself has kept her in the underlying belief that she is weak, and she is always on constant alert for the possibility that someone might take advantage of her. It is, by her account, exhausting.

She has allowed herself to be defined by this moment in her life. For years, she has felt somehow damaged because of this event. Every day, no matter what happens, her first thought or filter is how is this impacted by what has happened to me. She acknowledges that she has many redeeming qualities. She is a good friend, a great mother, a successful businesswoman, active in the community, and an all-round great person. Despite all this, she still feels an undercurrent of being bad or less than for allowing this to happen to her.

Like so many people, Marcia has a willingness to forgive herself and can see the value in it but has no idea how to go about it. Repeating over and over "I forgive myself" certainly hadn't worked, she says.

Do you have some "bad" in your past that you allow to define you?

Consider the following steps, adapted from Fred Luskin's book, *Forgive For Good* (2003), as you begin the process of forgiving yourself or another.

1. Know exactly how you feel about what happened and be able to articulate what about it was not okay. Then tell a few trusted people about your experience.

2. Make a commitment to yourself to do what you have to do to feel better. Forgiveness is for you and not for anyone else. This is the good news and the bad news. The choice is entirely yours.

3. Forgiveness does not necessarily mean reconciliation with the person that hurt you or condoning of their action. Forgiveness can be defined as the "peace and understanding that come from blaming that which has hurt you, taking the life experience less personally, and changing your grievance story."

4. Get the right perspective on what is happening. Recognize that your primary distress is coming from the hurt feelings, thoughts, and physical upset you are suffering now, not what offended you or hurt you two minutes or ten years ago. Forgiveness helps to heal those hurt feelings.

5. At the moment you feel upset, practice a simple stress-management technique to soothe your body's flight or fight response.

6. Give up expecting things from other people that they are never going to give you. Recognize what "unenforceable rules" you have or what rules you have for how others must behave. Remind yourself that you can create love, health, peace, and prosperity and do what it takes to get them.

7. Put your energy into looking for another way to get your positive goals met than through the experience that has hurt

you. Instead of mentally replaying your hurt, seek out new ways to get what you want.

8. Remember that a life well lived is the best revenge. Instead of focusing on your wounded feelings, and thereby giving the person who caused you pain power over you, learn to look for love, beauty, and kindness around you. Forgiveness is about personal power. When you forgive, you take back your power.

9. Amend your grievance story to remind yourself of the heroic choice you made to forgive.

Forgiveness also takes place in layers. Depending on the level of insult and how pervasive it is to your being, it can takes weeks, months, or years to forgive. If you are willing to be active in the process of forgiveness instead of just letting time pass, you will inevitably have more success, less pain, and create more happy memories. Use the list above to help you be active in the process. It is important to remember that forgiveness is a practice in the same way that gratitude is. Practicing forgiveness leads to healthy relationships as well as a healthier body. It also influences our attitude, which opens our heart to kindness, beauty, and love instead of anger, sadness, and revenge.

It's important to remember that forgiveness is often a two-way street. On the one hand, there is the forgiveness of the offender, but for those who blame themselves for allowing whatever has happened must also deal with forgiving themselves. Sometimes there is so much focus on anger, blame, or hatred towards the offender that it takes a long time to recognize the need to forgive themselves. I am certainly no stranger in learning to forgive myself. For a large portion of my life, I strove to be perfect so that I would be loved. I didn't know at the time that there was another choice. Imagine my surprise when I finally realized that the concept of perfect was as mutable and changing as the weather—being perfect for my family meant one thing, being perfect for my friends another, and for my partner yet another set of self-imposed rules. It was a constant balancing act in which I could never quite keep all the plates spinning at once.

One life-changing day, I was having a casual conversation with someone, and in the context of the conversation, it became so clear to me how I had held myself captive for most of my life by not being willing or able to forgive myself for my imperfections. Truthfully, forgiving myself had never even occurred to me. In my world, the way that I got love was to be the best student and the best athlete—bring home the trophies and make them proud. There was no such thing as forgiveness, only doing better.

When I first entertained the concept of self-forgiveness I had a whole host of confusing thoughts swirling in my brain. I had always thought that all those wrongs had to be stored for safekeeping, locked deep inside so that I would never let it happen again. Wow, did I miss the mark on that one! Storing all those wrongs and never forgiving myself just made me more imperfect and undeserving of love. It was, of course, no accident that at the time I had inevitably sought people in my life who were essentially emotionally and physically unavailable, selfish, and fairly incapable of truly loving at any more than a superficial level.

As I began really working with this concept in earnest, I dragged up as many of the memories of things that I believed I had done wrong. One-by-one, I reframed the incident to see myself with compassion and as someone who truly did have her heart in the right place with good intentions but made mistakes—mistakes that fortunately, in hindsight, were the birthplace of growth, passion, and direction. As I continued to follow this thread, an entirely new awareness blossomed within me. I began to really understand the saying that "we are spiritual beings having a human experience." I had heard this many times before but always considered it a nice, profound saying that went in one ear and out the other.

One interesting thing that revealed itself in the process of my self-forgiveness was learning that I needed to forgive myself for not allowing myself to be fully me. After all, I was the only one who was in charge of how I lived my life. Choosing to live it in fear or making life choices based on being loved or approved of never worked, but I chose them anyway. Each choice diminished my essence even further, and I became less and less my true self and more of what I believed or thought others wanted from me.

I sort of accidentally stumbled across this understanding when I was having a conversation with a friend who was trying to figure out whether she was gay or not. She believed that she was gay, but she was terrified of the response that she would get from her family and friends. She felt that everyone would find her a fraud and judge her for not being real and would question whether she could be trusted or not. She dreaded being cut off from family, friends, or business associates and was sitting on the fence as to whether it was easier to live a lie or have the courage to be herself.

I said, "I think the only person who will be judging you for not being real will be you. You have been fighting within yourself for a long time, and you are judging yourself for not making the choice to follow your heart and soul's desires. No one worth having as a friend will judge you for following your heart. Choosing not to step into your true self will not make this easier. That you can be certain of." They say that we teach best what we need to learn most, and in that moment, the proverbial two-by-four hit me square in the head and I began the process of forgiving myself and had one of the best a-ha moments of my life: It's impossible to live in your sweet spot without being yourself.

In reality, my friend's family and coworkers adore her and never would have considered abandoning her for her being gay. When she finally did gather her courage and told her family, they were curious, reassuring, loving, and accepting. Her business partners never batted an eye and one even responded with "cool." She will tell you that she is happier in her life than she has ever been and that letting go of self-judgment is what allowed her to begin to step into her authentic self.

Another funny thing happened on the way to writing this forgiveness chapter. I did my normal research, being mindful to include all aspects of spirit, mind, and body that I could find. I also asked everyone I could about their experiences with forgiveness, and what emerged for me was the realization of how many of us hold ourselves back and down because of the things that we have done in our lives. Most were clearly lacking a sense of self-compassion. Instead of acknowledging that we were being the best people we could be at the time, we often use the offense as one more notch in our belts of how not good enough we are.

Sometimes the inability to forgive yourself has you riding a tide and you don't even know you are on the boat. Ariel is a beautiful wise woman in her midfifties. She told me that in her midthirties she had had an affair with a married man whom she loved deeply. She explained that she hadn't planned for it to happen, but he had treated her in a way that she had never been treated, and her heart opened in ways she never thought possible or had even imagined. She had had only two significant relationship experiences up until this point and, as she puts it, "was fairly ignorant in the ways of the heart."

As is the case with many affairs, it ended badly, leaving her filled with shame and remorse. As she began the process of understanding what had happened, she was filled with regret for having been "that woman." Prior to this, she had had strong judgments against people who had affairs and now she was one of them. She pushed intimate relationships in her life away, believing herself to be unworthy. As time passed, she was able to allow for relationships but they were always with people who were either unavailable or unable to fully commit to the relationships, which were generally short lived. Many years went by, and she eventually sought the help of a therapist with the intention of figuring out why she was so angry.

As she began to whittle away at the layers of her anger, she realized that she was angry with herself for what she thought was the mistake of her life that would tarnish her forever. In time, she learned that the man she had been in love with had returned to his wife, and they were able to face their issues and strengthen their relationship as a result of the affair. Likewise, her heart opened up in a way that she had never even known was possible. Little by little, she began to accept that they were both still the good people they were to begin with but had, for whatever reasons, chose this opportunity to learn these lessons in this way. Condemning herself to a loveless life for this mistake served no one. She was finally able to forgive herself when she understood that she was a really good human who learned a really tough lesson. Nothing more.

What was essential for Ariel to forgive herself was to understand that self-forgiveness is totally linked to self-compassion. Self-compassion is recognizing that you were doing the best you could at the time whatever happened occurred. Looking back later and saying I could have, would have, or should have serves no purpose except to punish yourself for what you didn't do. The reality is you did whatever you did. It's over and it is in the past. It is only the understanding that you gained by making the mistake that allows you in hindsight to make the could have, should have, and would have statements. Recognize that making mistakes is the birthplace of learning and essential to acceptance. Just like I tell my daughter, "Get comfortable with mistakes because they are part of life and you're going to make a ton of them in your life." Mistakes do not make you a good or bad person. It is the energy you assign to them as a result of making them that defines how much compassion you will allow for yourself.

Radical Forgiveness by Colin Tipping and *Forgive for Good* by Fred Luskin are two excellent books that I can recommend if you want to delve further into the process of forgiveness. They approach the same information from different perspectives and will give you the opportunity to consider other aspects of forgiveness. Being able to forgive, whether it is yourself or others is essential for living in your sweet spot. In the words of Lewis Smedes, "To forgive is to set a prisoner free and discover that the prisoner was you."

Chapter 7

Compassion

There but for the grace of God go I.
– John Bradford

Not long ago, there was a mother in the news who was charged with murder. Normally, her husband took their child to daycare, but he had a doctor's appointment and would have been pressed to get there on time, so she offered to do it for him. Besides being a thoughtful mother and wife, she is an all-around good human.

She strapped her young son in the car seat and off they went. As many children do, her son fell asleep as they made their way across town. In the silence, the mother found her mind wandering and thinking about her day and what she needed to get done. Absentmindedly and on autopilot she drove straight to her office and forgot her soundly sleeping son in the back seat. She parked her car, grabbed her briefcase and purse, locked the car, and proceeded into her office, leaving her son in the car in the hot June heat. As you can imagine, tragically, her son died very shortly after that.

Judgment is often the initial response for most when something like this happens. We wonder how could she forget her son? How could she have let this happen? Compassion is considering the other side of the story. Mistakes happen, and in this case, the results were tragic. She not only lost her son, but her own life as she knew it as well. Yes, technically she was alive but void of any emotion other than grief and shock. Not to mention the devastation her husband was suffering. He lost his son and his relationship with his wife, as she was now in jail. What feelings does this story provoke in you? Are you experiencing outrage that a mother didn't protect her son or are you feeling compassion for a mistake that resulted in the devastation of this family's life?

Compassion is simply the feeling of empathy for others. It is how you think about what has happened to others and the meaning you assign it. When we can identify with our fellow humans and see them as an extension of ourselves, we associate that what has happened to them could possible happen to us. In this way, we attempt to understand what they are feeling and how we would respond given a similar situation. When we don't have compassion, we begin to see our fellow humans as not us. This thinking is what allows for conflict in the Middle East, girls to be stolen in Nigeria, or even our own issues with immigration. Dehumanizing people allows us to forget that they too are mothers, fathers, sons, daughters, brothers, and sisters.

Choosing compassion over judgment is essential for living in your sweet spot. The Dalai Lama says that "Compassion is a necessity, not a luxury, and without it humanity cannot survive." When we identify with others, we are motivated to do something to help them. Without it we avoid, judge, or ignore other's issues. Humans are wired for connection and having compassion is one of the ways that we develop that connection. To be able to put yourself in another's situation and have an understanding of what they are going through while not judging is essential for creating the space for that connection to occur.

There is a general consensus by those who study compassion that there are three requirements one must feel in order to have compassion:

1. People have to know that the people they are witnessing didn't cause their own suffering intentionally.

2. People have to be able to self-identify and picture themselves with the same issue.

3. People have to identify with the fact that what the people are suffering from is of a serious nature and significant to them.

While compassion for others is important, it is equally significant to have compassion for yourself. As children, many of us were given negative messages or suffered traumatic events, which we assigned meaning to. As we move through our lives, these concepts and beliefs that were formed live in the background of our subconscious and affect the way we live our lives and the choices we make. For example, if you were a child who lived in a household with a narcissistic parent and were consistently told to be seen and not heard, the younger part of you is essentially conditioned to minimize your place in the world. As you age and begin living your own life, you take risks in asking for what you want and by being seen, but often the fear you have may seem out of proportion. It's important to have compassion for yourself and remember that the younger side of you has been conditioned to stay small. Having compassion for the younger side of yourself in those moments will help you get through them. If you live your life beating yourself up, it is critical to find whatever way works for you to curtail this behavior because it is virtually impossible to live in your sweet spot without self-compassion.

Our childhood shapes the way we live as adults. As we progress closer to our authentic selves, certain beliefs that we formed erroneously need to be brought to the surface and assigned new meaning. Having compassion for the younger side of you and what you endured is an important part of healing that must be addressed. I truly believe that all of us were masterfully ingenious in the way we adapted and learned to survive. There comes a time when those solutions no longer serve us and often hold us back. Having compassion for that part of you will help you to move forward to create healthy and successful ways to communicate and create.

Many children learn from an early age that being critical is the only way to get results. We watched our parents do it and learned to do it ourselves. Unfortunately, not as many are taught that being kind to themselves is the way to achieve any measure of success. Dr. Kristen Neff, an associate professor at the University of Texas, has done extensive research on compassion and the way we treat our fellow humans and ourselves. This research has shown that when we criticize ourselves, it generally serves no purpose but to lower our self-esteem and promote anxiety, especially as it relates to success, which often leads to depression.

It makes sense if you think about it. How many times has berating yourself worked to get anything done? Saying to yourself, "I'm an idiot," "I'm so fat," or "I'm such a slacker" makes you feel bad about yourself but rarely works to get the job done or make any long-lasting changes. Dr. Neff has authored the book *Self-Compassion: The Proven Power of Being Kind to Yourself* (2011), which is a great read, especially if you are someone who has difficulty acknowledging your positive attributes. In her book, she states that self-compassion consists of three components:

- *Self-kindness*: This is the capacity to be gentle and kind to yourself when you are suffering. Being mean to yourself never serves any purpose but to hold you back and keep you down.

- *Mindfulness*: This involves being able to practice being in the present moment. It means being able to observe, without judgment, the moment you are in and not attach it to any past failure or perceived future outcome.

- *Common Humanity*: This is the recognition that every one of us has struggles. The type of struggle may vary from one person to another, but it is critical to recognize that we are not alone or the only ones who fail, makes mistake, experience loss or feel rejected. It is what bonds us as humans.

These three components provide the opportunity for us to move into a place where we can openly deal with the pain we are experiencing. Otherwise, we often feel shame, which breeds secrecy, causing us to hide the truth from others and ourselves. The old saying "the truth will set you free" is very accurate in this case because when we are able to tell ourselves the truth of what we are really feeling, we are able to process it and move through it much quicker.

Despite the fact that the three components of compassion seem kind, gentle, and humanitarian, self-compassion sometimes gets a bad rap and some judge others as having self-pity or being egocentric. This couldn't be further from the truth. Dr. Neff dispels this myth by stating that self-compassion is nothing more than seeing things as they are. This means that we don't assign it some meaning—"I'm such a loser," "I'm an idiot," "I never get anything right," etc. It is simply noticing that you are hurting, while recognizing, at the same time, that others also have similar issues. Self-compassion does not separate you. In fact, it is usually the shame that accompanies the negative thought patterns that separate us more. Having compassion for yourself actually brings you closer to recognizing and having compassion for others. It is very difficult to know how someone feels if you haven't felt it yourself. When you are able to say to your friend, partner, or child, "I understand how you feel. I know you are in pain," you actually deepen your connection to each other, bringing you closer together. Often creating the space for intimacy in this way creates an opening for further discussion, creating vulnerability, and helping you move through the pain more quickly.

How many of you have used self-criticism to motivate you at some point in your life? How's it worked so far? When you say things to yourself like "I never do it right. I'll never lose weight. I am always messing things up," you further reinforce your negative state and, when it doesn't serve to motivate you, then you feel worse and this puts you on an endless cycle of not good enough, failure, and criticism. Undeniably, it doesn't work for anyone. It serves only to tear down and minimize you, which increases the likelihood of failure. Dr. Neff states, "There's actually nothing motivating about criticizing yourself, because it makes you fear failure and lose faith in yourself. Even if you do achieve great things, you're often miserable anyway." For some, when they do achieve some measure of success, they don't enjoy it because they feel like it was just luck or a fluke.

Often those who were criticized as children assume the role of self-criticizer as adults. No longer having a parent around to motivate them by being critical, they pick up the slack and criticize themselves. It is what they learned and what they eventually come to believe about themselves. Some use self-criticism as a way to protect themselves or get what they need. By going on the offensive and criticizing themselves, they avoid the pain inflicted by those who berate them. It also serves to separate them from the deep pain of shame they feel that was brought about by the criticism in the first place. This is especially true for those who grew up in an environment where a mistake meant punishment. Self-criticism is a way to prevent consequences. It didn't work then, and it won't work now. Consider observing your thoughts and messages that you say to yourself for just a day. It is important that you do so from a place of pure observation and no judgment. It is for information only. Notice whether they are positive, loving, supportive thoughts or are whether they are minimizing and self-critical. If you find you are fairly critical of yourself try to begin to catch your thoughts as you recognize them and reverse it with a positive statement. It will take practice and you won't believe yourself initially, but over time, as you continue to give your cells a different message, you will create new neurological pathways and begin to think differently. Living in your sweet spot requires that we end the self-criticizing and find constructive ways to motivate ourselves.

Mike's father was unpredictable. He never knew which side of his dad's personality was going to show up. What he did know was that if he could figure out what counted as "good behavior" in the moment, he could avoid being punished. The problem was that the rules changed. What was appropriate behavior one day became unacceptable the next. Throughout his childhood, Mike was constantly on the alert to figure out what made his father happy, which, as you can imagine, he was never successful at. Mike came to believe that the way to get love and approval was to figure out what people wanted and give it to them.

He would often say to himself, "What an idiot. I should have known she didn't want to go," "I hate that I didn't figure that out sooner," "How many times am I going to have to go through this until I learn," or "I should have known he/she wanted that." Consistently focusing on what others want leaves you out of the equation, making it difficult for you to know what you want. In Mike's case, he was taught that thinking about oneself was selfish, and he had tremendous resistance to allowing for the possibility that what he wanted was important.

As humans, we often have resistance to change. It can be scary, especially if you have used your behavior to avoid feeling pain. Recognizing when you are in significant resistance to something is a good clue that you are going against the grain of a childhood message that, in all likelihood, you use to hold yourself back.

Resistance is opposition, and, whenever opposition is present, it is because you either don't want to do it, don't believe you can do it, don't want to expose yourself, or, at some point, you were told you shouldn't do it. This resistance often reveals itself in subtle ways, but being able to recognize what you do can be invaluable in understanding the mischief you do to keep yourself from having what you want. Resistance often shows up as irritability, fear, feeling discomfort, anger, isolation, superiority, etc. As you can see, resistance is sneaky and disguises itself, but being able to get in a place of curiosity is a way to uncover whatever it is you are avoiding. Stop in a moment of discomfort and be present to what you're feeling, then say to yourself, "Wow, I seemed to be really... (angry, sad, depressed, enrage, etc.) for no obvious reason. I wonder what this is about?" Then follow the thread to figure out what is going on underneath, which will help you understand what you are resisting. Avoiding judgment of yourself for having the emotion will allow you to understand the emotion with minimal pain.

The following story illustrates how important recognizing and having compassion for your younger self is in being able to create your dreams as an adult. Eliza is an incredibly talented artist who was an accountant for the majority of her adult life. Through a series of events, she was able to muster the courage to quit her job and indulge full-time in her passion of creating paintings. She worked diligently to accumulate enough pieces for her big debut. She was very excited but, at the same time, had a nagging fear looming in the background that she continually pushed down and tried to ignore. She had just three more paintings that she had to put the finishing touches on, and she would be ready.

In an effort to support Eliza's need for some concentrated time to finish, her friends graciously offered her a week at their beach house so she could get away from the hustle and bustle of family life with the kids and her husband, and finish the paintings. Her husband fully supported the idea, and she jumped at the chance. Excitedly, she packed all of her supplies and partially finished paintings in her SUV and headed off to the beach with her dog Mitsy in tow.

Arriving at the beach after the long drive and then unloading, she decided to take a walk on the beach to stretch her legs and unwind before she got started on her work. As she strolled down the beach, she could feel her hectic life slipping away and began to relax, enjoying the waves and breeze and feeling excited about the freedom she would have for the next week. Returning from her walk, as she climbed the stairs to the house, she decided to go to the grocery store and stock up so that she wouldn't have to take time to go out to eat, leaving more time to do her work. Returning from the grocery store, she felt too tired to start painting and hadn't set up yet anyway, so she decided to make a good dinner, take another walk on the beach with the dog, and turn in early to get a fresh start in the morning.

Drinking coffee on the front porch in the morning, she realized that she was much more tired than she thought and decided, with a little guilt, to take the day to just be lazy, enjoy the pool, take a bike ride, and walk on the beach. Rationalizing that, "If I am rested, I will be more creative, get more done in less time, and be more present." Lazy she was. For the next three days, she repeated the same pattern, only adding reading a book and a bottle of wine to the "resting." When her husband called and asked how things were going she responded, "slow."

On the fourth day with her paintings, easel, and materials just inside the front door where she had left them, she began to wonder, "What's going on here? If I didn't know better, I'd think I was trying to avoid getting these pictures done, but I know that's not true." Lying in her beach chair for yet another "rest" day, she started to think about the upcoming debut and how she was feeling about putting her work out there. "What if it's a total flop and people don't like my work? What if they criticize my work and question why I am even doing this?"

One by one, her deep-seated fears floated to the surface, and she could hear her dad's voice in her head. "Don't draw attention to yourself. Nobody likes a show-off. You can't make any money at art. Get a real job and put this foolishness behind you. Who do you think you are, Picasso?"

Basking in the hot sun, her mind drifted back to her childhood with flashes of her father's defeating messages. She was transported to a memory when she was eight years old and had proudly drawn a series of pictures, hung them all from strings, and then strung them up all over her room to create a museum. Her dad walked by her room, glanced in, and, being taken aback by all the mess, yelled at her, "Get that crap off the walls and make sure the tape doesn't pull the paint off." Feeling shame and defeat, she removed the pictures, crumpled them, and threw them in the trash.

Compassion for her younger self flooded her as tears welled up in her eyes. "No wonder I can't finish my paintings," she thought. "I'm still eight years old waiting for my father to approve of me. It's my eight-year-old self that is scared to death to put herself out there." Thinking of her own precious children made her feel even more compassion for her younger self. Clarity flooded her mind and a new energy filled her being. Rising from the beach chair, she went back into the house and, in the next two days, finished the three paintings. Despite having a successful debut with her work, she was always mindful and compassionate toward the eight-year-old inside her.

What messages were you given as a young child that prevent you from living your dreams? It was essential for Eliza, as it is for most of us, to allow for the time and space for these feelings to come up. We don't necessarily need a beach trip for this to occur, but it is important to stop the steady stream of stress and slow down enough to hear the pleadings of your higher self. Find whatever way works for you to listen to yourself. The answers are within; it's just a matter of getting them out. Once you find them, be sure to look at them with compassionate eyes.

Exercise

One thing to consider is that if there is something that you really want to do whether it's paint, write, learn to swim, play the guitar, or whatever, and you don't do it, there is probably some message that you were given that keeps you from achieving your goal. One possible way to begin to know what's holding you back from doing what you want is to try the following exercise:

> Write the sentence:
>
> If I (fill in the blank with something you want to do, such as learn to fly) then (write as many answers as you can make up).

So you may write something like: If I learn to fly, I might die, my family would disapprove, I'd be wasting a lot of money, I'd cross off one of my bucket lists, I'd be scared to death, my kids would think it was cool, etc. Even if the answers seem silly at first, write them down. In fact, I encourage you to be as creative as possible with your answers because the truth is that many of the reasons that we hold ourselves back are silly when they finally come to the surface. Taking the power back that we gave away as children is what allows us to create what we want as adults.

Chapter 8

Learning to Say "I Want"

If you don't go after what you want, you'll never have it. If you don't ask, the answer is always no. If you don't step forward, you're always in the same place.
–Nora Roberts

What do you want?" Interestingly, I have found that answering that question is difficult for many people. It seems on the surface that it should be a no-brainer, but in reality, our brains go through a multilevel filtering process to evaluate not only what we might want but also whether it is permissible to say, "I want." Unfortunately, it's almost impossible to live our authentic lives without being able to say I want. If you are not free to say I want to go to school, be a race car driver, be a fireman, or paint pictures you cannot possibly begin to do what it is that you want to do. So many people become what they are or what they do because they were told to since it made sense, it made more money, it was better for the family, they were good at it, or it satisfied someone else's dream that was never realized.

Frequently, early in childhood we are given the message that asking for what we want is selfish. These early messages may have included statements such as "Life isn't always about what you want," "Life doesn't revolve around you," "Why don't you think about what [he, she, I, they] want for a change?" Any of these sound familiar?

115

Certainly, our parents were not malicious in their intent. They were simply teaching what they had been taught in the way they were taught. No one would argue that thinking and doing for others is unimportant, but equally important is being able to assess what it is that your own heart desires. It is what shapes our destiny, helps us decide where we will live, what we want to do for a living, who or if we will marry, and how many children we may or may not want to have. It even involves something as basic as how and what we want to eat.

Recently I attended a continuing education conference and, while waiting for the course to begin, struck up a conversation with the doctor sitting next to me. He was a recent graduate, and instead of being filled with excitement and anticipation toward starting his new life, he was paralyzed with fear.

"Do you mind if I ask you how you decided where and how you wanted to practice?" he asked. "I am trying to figure out whether I want to practice in a group, be a solo practitioner, have other disciplines in the office, or just go work for someone else. I don't even think I know where I want to live. I'm so stuck, I haven't done anything and it's freaking me out. Everyone is pressuring me to get on with it, but I don't know where to start or what I want. I don't want to make a mistake. It's such a big decision."

I reassured him that most graduates in all professions go through some form of anxiety trying to figure out the next step once they have completed their studies. I suggested he try making a pro and cons list to help clarify his options concretely in black and white. I shared with him, "Trust that no matter what choice you make, if you find it isn't right, you can change your mind and pick again. If you put yourself in a situation with another practitioner and recognize that it isn't for you, you can pick another option. Nothing is set in stone." I assured him that if he gave himself permission to make a choice, even if it proves to be a mistake, it would be the right choice in that moment. If nothing else, making the wrong choice would give him clarity about what he did want. I also asked him to consider making a list of what he would do if money, location, and people were not an issue and create from that space.

I could visibly see his body relax with the freedom of being able to change his mind. "That feels a whole lot more doable and realistic. Thanks," he said. The next day as he was walking in and passed by, he smiled and said, "Got my list together last night. Think I'm going to be okay."

There are many reasons that people have difficulty asking for what they want. For some, asking for what they want means drawing too much attention to themselves and is not worth the exposure. For others, the fear of rejection keeps them from saying "I want." It is easier to avoid asking than risk being hurt or facing the reality that they wouldn't give it to you anyway.

Others believe asking for what they want will obligate them to return the favor, and they don't want to have to owe anyone anything. Still others would just prefer that you already know what they want and expect you to give it to them without asking. This is often accompanied by some overt or covert punishment because you should have already known what they wanted. Unfortunately, there are also those who believe themselves to be too unworthy to even think about what they want, much less ask.

Throughout the year, I do many workshops and lectures. One of the things I discuss is how your thoughts create chemical messages, how those chemicals affect each of your cells, and, in turn, how you live your life. When you don't take responsibility to say, "I want," your cells have no direction to help you create what it is you desire. If you don't take an active role in the process of creating your life, then the default becomes what someone tells you to do, what you think you should do, or nothing happens at all. All the cells in your body participate in this process in one way or the other, and the thoughts you think have a significant impact on the happiness you experience. When you are not specifically directing your thoughts to create what you want, you often end up creating what you don't want or are not satisfied with what you do create.

Almost without exception, after each presentation, I will have one or two people who will email and say that they loved the information, and it really made a lot of sense, but they needed help figuring out what they wanted. My first thought was, "How could I possibly begin to know what they want?" However, as time went on and I continued to have similar requests, I began to have some understanding about how much of a problem asking for what you want really can be for some.

Ask yourself where you fall on the "I want" meter? Are you able to say I want? Can you ask your husband, wife, boss, or friends for what you want? Do you even know what you want? If not, determine what it is that stands in your way and, when appropriate, begin to take risks to ask for or express what your heart desires. One way of doing this is to pick a category such as a job for example. Assume there are no restrictions and write down everything that you would want in that job. Then go back and look at the list and ask yourself what do you tell yourself about why you can't have it. Do you tell yourself you're not smart enough, don't have the right connections, nobody would hire you or you are female/ male, or something else? We all tell ourselves why we can't have something to keep from being disappointed. The problem is that it doesn't work and more often than not, we use it as a way of avoiding taking responsibility for creating what we do want.

In general, people really do want to help out and give you what you want. Frequently, they will avoid offering to help because you are unable to tell them what you want and they don't want to make a mistake and give, or do, something you don't want. Think about the last time you wanted to help a sick friend or someone who had suffered the loss of a loved one. Did you avoid doing something for them because you didn't know what to do, or did you avoid doing something because they didn't know what they wanted and couldn't ask? One way to approach this is by saying, "I know you may not know what you need, but when a thought comes to mind, I really want to help and would love for you to ask me."

There's a story about a husband and wife who were sitting eating dinner. The husband was visibly irritated, and despite his wife's repeat-edly asking what was wrong, he continued to say "Nothing." Eventually her husband exhaled a big sigh, rose from his seat, and grabbed the salt and banged it on the table as he sat back down. Looking at her, he said, "If you really loved me you would have known I wanted the salt without my having to ask." His wife sat there dumbfounded. "What does love have to do with the salt?"

Now on the surface, I know this seems like a silly story, but in reality this type of experience happens every day and exemplifies how some avoid responsibility for asking what they want by making it someone else's job. In this way, anything that goes wrong is not their fault, and they can blame their lack on their loved ones. This type of interaction is not limited to interpersonal relationships. It happens every day in the business world as well. Instead of your boss being able to say, "You should have had that report to me by five," when it doesn't arrive, you are at fault because you should have known that he/she wanted it today. Then there are those who want a project to be done in a specific way with certain information included and have an expectation that you should know that, and when it doesn't happen, it becomes your fault.

Another aspect that often gets in the way of asking for what you want is guilt. There are some people who feel guilty about asking for what they want because they were taught that having enough meant you shouldn't want anything more, even if it was something different. Mary's mom was an incredibly generous person whose whole life revolved around giving to others. She always volunteered at school, the church, the Red Cross, and wherever she was needed. The rest of her life was dedicated to her family. She rarely had time for or asked for anything for herself. As Mary grew up and watched her mother's dedication to others, she found it difficult to give anything to herself. Anytime Mary would ask for something, her mom would gently say, "Do you really need that? Don't you think you have enough? There are a lot of people who would give anything to have what you have." As a result, Mary still finds it difficult to buy anything for herself without feeling guilty.

There are some who devise clever ways to get what they want without asking, which is also known as manipulation. Gina and Beth both work for a consulting firm that is next to a spa. The spa has a talented massage therapist whom many people in the office use. As it happened, Beth and Gina were both scheduled for a massage on the same afternoon, one following the other. Beth was at four o'clock and Gina at five. Gina had a dinner party that night at seven and had to allow for time to get home, shower, dress, and get across town. She was feeling pressed for time, but really wanted a massage, so she gave some thought to how she might get Beth to switch with her.

Gina went into Beth's office at about three-thirty and said, "You'd better get going. Don't you have a massage at four?"

Smiling, Beth responded, "Gina, it's next door. I'm pretty sure I'll make it."

Gina persisted. "I know, but he always runs overtime with you."

"He runs overtime with everybody, which is one more reason I don't need to leave yet. I have a few things to finish, and I want to clean this up, and besides, I still have plenty of time. Less time now by the way since I have had to stop and talk to you," she joked. "What's this about? Why are you bugging me about leaving?"

"I'll cleanup for you, if you leave now," Gina responded.

"What is it that you really want? Because I can't remember you ever offering to cleanup for me in the seven years we have worked together."

"Well, if you want more time I can take the four and you could take the five o'clock," Gina offered.

"Thanks, but I have things to do later, so the four is better for me," replied Beth. Gina huffed, turned on her heel, and hurried out angrily without saying anything, leaving Beth totally confused.

Taking responsibility to ask for what you want saves time and energy, in addition to keeping your integrity with yourself and others. If Gina had initially asked Beth to switch with her, she could have avoided all the extra time and energy it took to try to get Beth to switch, and in this case, it didn't work anyway.

Some people stop asking for what they want because they believe they will never get it anyway, so why bother to ask. This was particularly true for Peter. He was an avid tennis player, and his birthday was coming up in the next month. He wanted a new tennis racquet and his

121

parents agreed that they would get it for him for as a birthday present. Tennis was Peter's life, and he played all the time. Getting a new racquet was a big deal. He went to the pro at the club where he played and took out several racquets to demo to get a feel for each one and how it affected his stroke. After playing with more than a dozen racquets, he narrowed it down to two and played with each one of them for hours. Finally, he made his decision on the racquet and then agonized over the string selection. When all the decision-making was complete, he excitedly went to his parents and told them, "I want this racquet with these strings." Without looking up, his father kept reading the paper and nodded, saying "Okay, Peter."

The big day came and Peter was so excited. He was going to use his new racquet in a tournament that he was playing in that weekend, and he just knew it was going to make a difference in his play. His parents handed him his perfectly wrapped present as Peter beamed. Of course, he knew what it was, but he was still filled with anticipation. He slowly unwrapped the present, and when he looked down, he couldn't believe it, it was not the racquet he had chosen.

"Why didn't you get me the racquet I told you I wanted?" he asked.

His father said, "Well, son, this is a much better racquet, and we felt that since you were playing so much, you should have the best. We didn't feel that you knew what that was, so we went to the pro at the tennis center across town and asked him."

Peter was crestfallen. He could not believe that after all the effort to find the perfect racquet his parents totally ignored him. He had tried that racquet, and it was far too stiff for him. They hadn't even asked his coach which racquet would be best. Essentially, it was if they had said, "You aren't capable of knowing what you want, so we decided for you." They went across town and asked a total stranger who didn't even know him or how he played. He continued to use his old racquet and never asked his parents for anything again.

Have you ever been disappointed when you have risked asking for what you want? If so, how did it impact you? Does it have any effect on your ability to ask for anything now?

Sometimes when people spend energy deciding, researching, taking risks, and then ask and are denied, they stop asking from that point on. For some, it becomes a defining moment of "I'll never get what I want." When you do this, you hand over the power to shape your life to a situation and/or a person. You abdicate responsibility and make them responsible for what you don't have. In this way, it becomes their fault for what you don't have. Peter could have taken responsibility for his situation by asking his parents if he could take it back and get what he wanted, saving his money and buying his own racquet, or selling the new racquet and then buying the one he wanted. In not doing any of this, he doesn't get what he wants and makes it his parents fault. We all get hurt and disappointed. It is part of being human. It is what we do with that hurt that defines how much responsibility we are willing to take for our own happiness.

We have spent most of this chapter focusing on the reasons people are or are not able to say I want. Equally important is what the world misses out on when someone chooses not to say, "I want." When we ignore the pleadings of our souls, we hold the world back from knowing who we are and the gifts we have to offer. What if Lincoln hadn't been able to say, "I want to end slavery." What if Steve Jobs hadn't been free to say, "I want to make computers." Not to mention, what tennis would be like if Serena and Venus Williams hadn't been free to say, "I want to play tennis?"

When you don't or can't say, "I want," you hold yourself back from the world and from yourself. It doesn't matter what you do; it matters that you do. We all have our own unique contributions, and all are equally significant. Being able to say, "I want," is critical to the process, even if you are just saying it to yourself.

It's a little like playing baseball. When you're at the plate, you have five chances to do something with the ball. You can stand there waiting until the absolute perfect pitch comes, and when it doesn't, you strike out; you can take the walk; or you can work with whatever curveball or fastball you are thrown and say, "I want that one." My wish for you is that you want to knock it out of the park no matter what pitch you pick.

Chapter 9

Organization

When I first started writing, I knew I needed help. I had some old beliefs taking residence in my brain, courtesy of an English professor during my first year in undergraduate school. I can't remember exactly the verbiage she used, but the essence of it was that what I wrote was a waste of paper. So I decided to hire a writing coach with the hope that I could, at least, gain enough confidence to write newsletters for the patients I serve in my practice.

Through a series of events, I was put in contact with a coach named Kerri Richardson. We interviewed each other, and it seemed we were a good match. To get started, she sent me a welcome package that included a number of documents, one of which was a questionnaire that was designed in such a way that enabled her to know me better and assess my needs.

Most of the questions were pretty straightforward, but the first one gave me pause. The question was, "Name ten things that you have wanted to do in the past year, but haven't done." My first thought was I pretty much do everything I want to do. I literally could not think of one thing that I hadn't done that I wanted to do. I answered all the other questions and left that one blank. This needed some thought. As I spent time thinking about it throughout the day, truthfully I still couldn't come up with one thing that I hadn't done, let alone ten.

My phone rang, and it was a person who needed some information about an upcoming workshop that I was doing. I put her on hold and walked into my home office to retrieve the information that I knew had to be somewhere amongst the rubble. As I started to sift through piles, I thought, "Now here is something I have wanted to do for at least ten years and haven't done. Clean my office." I can't tell you the number of days or weekends that I had set aside to get organized, and each time something (anything) would take precedence.

I had my answer, and I got on a roll. The ten things I came up with were:

1. Clean my home office

2. Clean my personal office at work

3. Clean out the garage

4. Go through and remove all the clothes that no longer fit my daughter

5. Clean out my closet

6. Get rid of all the old books

7. Clean out the pantry

8. Renovate my treatment rooms

9. Clean out my closet

10. Get rid of the old woodpile in my yard

During my initial conversation with my coach, she asked what my impressions were of the questions that I had filled out. "Well, to tell you the truth, the first one sort of stumped me," I said, "because I pretty much always do what I want to do." She told me she had noticed that organization—more specifically, the lack of—clearly seemed to be the theme and asked what I thought that meant in terms of how I organize my life.

"I'm not sure," I said. "Every morning when I start my day, I think about what absolutely has to be done. If I get those things done, I feel like I have had a successful day, and the rest goes on the list for the next day." Then she asked what kind of message I thought that sent to the universe. I thought for a second, and I really couldn't think of anything except that clearly I was busy or overscheduled. So confessing that, I asked what she was getting at.

"Well," she said, "I think it sends a message to the universe that says, please don't give me one more thing to do. I can't handle what I have."

I was stunned at the truth of this statement. It was exactly how I was living my life. Always trying to catch up. I had become accustomed to two states of existence, comfortably behind and uncomfortably behind. This was not at all how I expected this coaching experience to go, but it was exactly what I needed in more ways than I yet knew.

I was then introduced to a fabulous tool called the Pomodoro Technique that would help me get organized without overwhelming me. I can't tell you the number of times that I truly wanted to get organized but the sheer magnitude of it stalled me from the start. It always proved to be a daunting and overwhelming task. After hours of sorting, it didn't seem that I had made a dent in whatever project I was working on. The Pomodoro Technique really worked and made all the difference in my success. There even is an app for it now that you can download on your smart phone.

With this technique, you first assign yourself a task. I decided on my piano. That may sound like an odd starting point, but my piano was covered on the top, keyboard, and seat with many neat piles of papers, which, aside from being a mess, also meant I could never play the piano. Once you have decided on your task, you begin working on it for twenty-five minutes. Research has been done to assess how much the brain can handle before it starts to get distracted. It turns out that for most, it is about twenty-five minutes. When the twenty-five minutes is up, you then step away from the task for five minutes. You can do anything you want for that five minutes, but not the task. As soon as the five minutes is up, you return to the task at hand for another twenty-five minutes. You continue this for a series of four rounds, or two hours. Most people can do two hours of anything without becoming overwhelmed. I had purchased a file cabinet, files, and a label maker before I got started, and in about four hours, my piano was mine again.

It took about a year, but I organized my entire house and office, and it has truly changed my life. It has allowed me space, time, and energy to live in my sweet spot and effortlessly enjoy the things I love doing. It has also created the space and time for creativity in ways I never even thought of. I have to confess that in no way would you have convinced me of this if I weren't living it. In my mind, I would have thought (and did) that it was nice for you, but it wasn't me. It always seemed that it was a project that if I had time someday I would get to it, but fortunately, my life was interesting enough that I had better things to do. Wow, did I get that wrong! If organization is an issue for you, I encourage you to try the Pomodoro Technique or any other organizational system.

I would never have believed that being organized could have made so much difference in my life if I hadn't experienced it firsthand.

128

Common sense told me being organized would help, and certainly, my environment would be more appealing, but I would never have guessed how much power would come from being organized. Honestly, I believe some part of me secretly rebelled against being organized. I'm not sure how I would have been labeled if I was organized, but it wasn't cool and I was sure it wasn't me. Looking back, I could never have imagined or even considered the difference it would make in my life. I don't give many guarantees, but I can guarantee that if you get organized it will change your life

Martin is a thirty-year-old, busy accounting executive who has been looking for a partner to get married and settle down with. He has had a number of promising dates, but as things progressed in the relationship, it eventually became apparent that something wasn't quite right. He never invited his prospective mates to his house and, at the end of an evening, always either spent the night at their houses or went home.

Eventually, Martin found the woman of his dreams, and they started to talk about marriage. She was bothered by the fact that he wouldn't take her to his house and would consistently badger and joke with him about it. He always replied that it just wasn't good enough for her. One day she said, "Why don't you just move if your house isn't good enough? If it isn't good enough for me, then surely it isn't good enough for you, and I know you make enough money to live somewhere nice. Is there something you're not telling me?"

In reality, the house was very nice, except when you opened the front door and witnessed the conditions he lived in. There were piles and boxes of things everywhere. He wasn't a hoarder, but feeling overwhelmed, he had never taken the time to get organized since moving in two years prior. This issue had caused him to lose more than one relationship, and he was sure he didn't want to lose this one. Finally, he confessed and told his soon-to-be wife that he was disorganized and ashamed of his house, and that's why he didn't want to bring her home.

"It can't be that bad," she said. Knowing how disorganized it actually was, he responded, "No, it's pretty bad."

"Well, why don't you get a professional organizer?" she said.

"There is such a thing?" he said, with an air of excitement in his voice. Relief flooded his body. To think that he could get rid of this albatross that he carried around and could pay someone to do it felt like magic. The next day he set up time with a professional organizer, and within a week, she had his house looking like a home. He created a romantic dining table, invited his prospective wife to dinner and, at the end, got down on one knee and asked her to marry him, to which she readily agreed. Ridding himself of the disorder in his life allowed him the freedom to pursue what he really wanted. Prior to this, he had no idea how much control being disorganized had over his life. If you have trouble getting started on your own, don't hesitate to hire a professional organizer. They not only help to get you organized but will also give you tools and techniques to keep you organized.

When you recognize the cost of being unorganized and the benefits generated from getting your life in order, you will find that the time and energy used to accomplish this more than pays for itself in dividends. Many studies have been done regarding the benefits of being organized, and throughout my research, I found consistency in the results. The findings revealed that with organization people had more time, as well as financial and emotional benefits.

Financially speaking, the average American has between $2,500 and $5,000 worth of perfectly usable stuff they aren't using. Interestingly, at the same time, they often carry $10,000 in credit card debt.

Consider how many of these purchases could have been avoided if they (or you) just went through the things that they already had. In addition to that, credit card companies collect a whopping seven billion dollars in late fees annually, and banks collect more than thirty-seven billion annually in overdraft fees. Certainly no one intentionally wants to reward the bank or credit card companies with extra money, yet every single month we do simply because we haven't taken the time to get organized to prevent it from occurring.

Another cost of disorganization to consider is that twenty-two billion dollars are spent on storage units each year. The monthly fee for storage units adds up quickly, and by the time you get around to sorting through and cleaning a unit out, you will have paid for the stored items several times over. The ironic thing is that when you finally do get around to cleaning out the storage unit, you will likely give away or donate the items. If it had been done initially, thousands would have been saved in storage fees, and a tax benefit from donations could have been possible. Consider donating to Goodwill or some other organization and receive a tax benefit. Goodwill has implemented a computerized system that makes it incredibly easy to keep track of your donations. Another lucrative option to reduce clutter is the Internet; eBay, Amazon, and Craigslist all have a proven track record as a way to resell items, reduce clutter, and make money. Yard sales are the tried and true conventional method of reducing large-scale excess in one fell swoop. What you don't sell, donate. Do not allow yourself the delusion that it will sell in your next sale. Get rid of it. It defeats the whole purpose to bring it back into your house.

There is also an often unrecognized and seldom discussed emotional component to disorganization. Depression can cause clutter and clutter can cause depression. Think of the last time that you cleaned something out or organized a space. Can you remember the feeling that went with it? Was it freeing? Did you feel empowered and expansive? Do you remember saying, "Sure felt good to get that done"? It's subtle and often taken for granted, but being organized feels good and is emotionally freeing.

Another example of cultural disorganization is that each year, millions of dollars go unclaimed from tax refunds and rebates because we aren't organized enough to keep the required information in an accessible place. Receipts are scattered or lost, credit card payments get missed, and critical documents are nowhere to be found. The government and banks love your disorganization and depend on it for a certain percentage of revenue each year, which they can statistically predict.

Let's consider taxes for a moment. How much of an emotional toll does it take on the average American taxpayer simply because he or she has to spend hours finding and pulling all the information together by the dreaded deadline? When you are organized, you put each piece of information in a specific tax folder as it accumulates throughout the year, and when the time comes to do the dreaded deed, you simply pull out the file and either do the taxes yourself or take it to an experienced tax person.

Many people underestimate or don't even consider home inventory as critical until there is a crisis and something important can't be found. For years, after each tax season, I would say to myself, "I'm going to get better about this and keep things together so I don't have to go through this next year." Despite my good intentions, I never did it until I realized the power of being organized.

It has been estimated that the average person spends about an hour daily looking for things. When you do the math, that adds up to two weeks every year, and by the age of fifty, you would have spent a year looking for things. Isn't that alone worth getting organized? Not to mention that in a poll 85% of couples said that besides money, the

next biggest issue that creates arguments is about clutter and disorganization.

Getting organized is easier than you think. Take it a step at time
and don't allow yourself to get overwhelmed before you start. Equally
important is having a system for maintaining your organization. My
home office was beautiful for about a month when the piles started
again. I am not diligent enough to file a piece of paper as soon as I
receive it, and deluding myself into believing that I would was a sure
way to set me up for failure. I solved the problem by putting a beautiful
inbox on my desk, and when it is full, I file. It takes about five minutes
and I need to do it every month or so. Being successful with organization involves finding a system that realistically suits you and doesn't
become another stressor. Living in your sweet spot is challenging if
your life is disorganized. Disorganization makes finding and following
your thread much more difficult and, at the very least, slows you down.
In fact, disorganization is often one of the ways that we hold ourselves
back and hide from the destiny we long for. This was certainly true in
my case. I hid behind being really busy for most of my life. It looked
like I was very productive, but in reality the busyness was limiting and
kept me from going for my dreams. After I was organized, there were
no more excuses for not writing, speaking, or giving workshops, all of
which I am passionate about, and at this point in my life, I can't
imagine not doing.

Look around your house or office with a critical eye, and see what
needs to be organized. When we look at our environments every day, it
is so easy to overlook what needs to be done. It is a background that
we become accustomed to. If you couple that with the fact that plowing
through it is the last thing you want to do, you can understand why day
in and day out we are disorganized everywhere we look.

Once you identify what needs to be done, I recommend that you
take a slow and steady pace with the organization process. Being over-

whelmed is a sure fire way to stall yourself out and keep yourself from even getting started, no matter how bothered you are by it. That was certainly true for me. I would pass by my home office wanting to reclaim it but was totally overwhelmed by the process. Now I can't image being disorganized again. When your life is organized, there is a peace and ease that underlies your existence. You will create, live, and love better. Get organized and watch for the magic it will bring to your life.

III. BODY
TAKING CARE OF
THE TEMPLE

Chapter 10

Putting Yourself in
the Equation

Where do you put yourself in your day? Seems like a funny question to ask. After all, aren't we all by the very nature of being alive, in our day? The reality is that very few of us actually take time out to dedicate some portion of the day totally for ourselves. It seems we can always find some excuse that trumps our belief that it's possible to have time for ourselves. The kids, the kids' schedules, the project at work, phone calls that have to be returned, groceries bought, dogs walked, dinner guests or just about any other realistic reason. There is no disputing there is an endless supply of things that demand our attention daily.

For the most part, it is highly unlikely that anyone will tell you to take time for yourself. Most people are usually consciously or unconsciously happy to have you slave away for them. Can you imagine your child saying to you, "Mom/Dad, you look tired. How about I mow the lawn or make dinner?" Or how about your boss saying, "You really have been working hard. How about you take some extra time at lunch or, better yet, take the afternoon off?" I'm not saying it doesn't happen, it's just unlikely.

Recently, I was talking to a woman about where she puts herself in her day, and she told me it was easier not to commit to doing something like that because she always felt bad when she didn't live up to her commitment. For her, taking time for herself meant working out regularly. To take a long run or go to the gym was a luxury that she rarely afforded herself.

I asked her if she realized that it wasn't a commitment to working out but a commitment to herself. I pointed out how committed she is to getting all her kids' needs met—volunteering at school, working a full-time, high-powered job, and running her household. She said, "It makes me exhausted when you say it like that." The truth is, she was exhausted. When we don't put ourselves in the equation, we get worn out and resentful, and over time, it affects our health, our relationships, and our ability to fully live our lives.

Balance is essential to good health and feeling alive, and making time for yourself is essential to that balance. It's no secret that we all have many things to do, and if we chose to, we could be busy almost all the time. In my life, I have come to accept that I am either comfortably behind or uncomfortably behind. There is no such thing as totally caught up. There is almost always something else to do. However, doing is not being. It can be as simple as taking time to sit down and read the paper, take a walk or a bath, meditate, or exercise. It doesn't matter what you do; it matters that you do it and consciously know that you are doing it for you. Take a minute and assess how well you do at putting yourself in your day.

Challenge yourself for a week to consciously put yourself in your day every day for at least half an hour and see what a difference it makes. I am confident that once you realize it can be done without your world falling apart, you will start claiming "me time" daily. It is also worth mentioning that by you taking time for yourself, you are teaching your kids and those around you that taking time for yourself is critical and expected. When your children see you taking time to meditate, take a walk, get a massage, or whatever you chose to do, you are setting an example about what it means to care for yourself. Whether we like it or not, children do learn what they live.

When we take time to stop the incessant chatter in our minds we can much more easily get in touch with who we are, what we want, and how we want to live. When we don't take the time we need, we blindly just carry on with the day-to-day minutia and life passes us by. When you take time for yourself, you will be happier, calmer, and more at ease. I can promise this will go a long way toward making your world run a whole lot smoother, and you will much more likely be living as your authentic self.

Chapter 11

Fueling the Engine

We can't possibly talk about living in the sweet spot without discussing the effects that food has on our lives. Over time, we have been exposed to numerous types of diets, fads, and programs, all purporting that this is the absolute best way to eat. We have been told to eat carbohydrates and avoid proteins. Then we were told to eat all the protein we want and avoid carbs. In addition, we had to sort out good fat from bad fat. The confusion is not ungrounded.

Back in the early eighties, the government became concerned about the rising levels of heart disease in our country, and it was believed that saturated fats were the culprits. So a new public health policy was initiated, and the surgeon general declared that it had been determined that excessive fat in the diet was the problem, and we were encouraged to minimize our fat intake. The problem was that low fat meant high carbohydrates.

I'm sure many of you remember when we were advised to eat whole wheat bread, multigrain cereals, pasta, etc. For many, including myself, this was sweet music to the ear, as most of us love our carbo-hydrates. So being dutiful citizens, we piled on the carbs.

A typical day might start with cereal, low-fat milk, and maybe a fruit followed by a lunch consisting of something such as a low-fat turkey sandwich on whole wheat bread. For dinner, you might consider some type of pasta dish, and if you were really trying to be healthy, you would put vegetables on it. Wow, did we get that one wrong! We ended up with a nation of incredibly fat people and the highest obesity rate in the world, accompanied by a phenomenal increase in cardiovascular disease and diabetes. So we tried again.

In 2011, the USDA (United States Department of Agriculture) introduced a new model, the MyPlate model, to address the alarming rate of obesity among Americans. We had all grown up with the pyramid as the gold standard for eating healthy. The problem was that it was confusing, and the number of people who truly under-stood it was limited. The fact is that it wasn't a good model anyway.

Even though MyPlate is easier to understand in that it shows how to put a plate of food together to make a balanced meal, it leaves out a lot of critical information. Instead of educating people about how and what to eat, we have once again lumped everyone in one category and set guidelines. It is not difficult to understand that it is probably going to be no more effective than the pyramids of the past.

If you look at the following image of MyPlate, you will see that it is suggested that you eat vegetables and grains in the same propor-tions, and that fruits and proteins should weigh in equally with the dairy all by its lonesome. Even though it is a better guideline than the pyramids of the past, it lacks critical information. For example, there is no stipulation that whole grains are better than refined grains, or what constitutes a protein

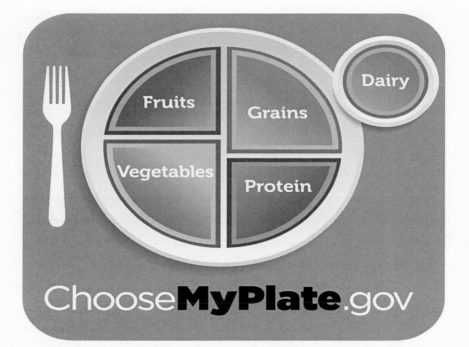

Figuring out what to eat is often very difficult and confusing. After experimenting with countless diets and working with thousands of patients, I have come to understand that everyone's food needs are different, and there is no one size fits all. This means that in order to find what your optimal food plan is, you will have to experiment, pay attention, and note the effect that each food has on you.

The following common guidelines safely apply to most people:

Balance is essential: In order to give your body the fuel it needs, eating a variety of different kinds of foods is critical. Avoid eating a diet of all protein, despite the fact that you may lose at little weight initially. In the long run, it does more harm than good. Eat different types of proteins, vegetables, and fats, varying the color and texture. A colorful plate is not only more appealing, it generally has more antioxidants and nutrients.

Know how food affects your body: It is essential that you pay attention to how you feel and how your body reacts when you eat a particular food in order to understand whether that food is healthy for you. Many people have food sensitivities that they are totally unaware of.

I suggest you keep a diet diary for a few weeks noting the foods you eat and how they affect you. It is an invaluable tool for gaining insight into how foods impact your body. Patients are consistently surprised when I have them do this exercise because most people make choices based on what looks good. What looks good isn't always what makes your body feel good. If you are someone who hasn't ever taken the time to do this, I believe you will gain a wealth of information about your relationship with food. Another fact is that often the foods that we crave are the very foods that we have sensitivities to, which is often what prevents people from making changes. I can't tell you the number of people who have said to me, "I'll give up most anything, but I'm not giving up my bread." It is, in essence, an addictive behavior. They know that it is detrimental to them but there is a rigid unwillingness to stop eating the food that betrays them.

A diet diary is a simple process that involves writing down the food you eat and then noting how your body reacts to the food. For example, if you had eggs and fruit for breakfast, which left you feeling good with no fatigue, gas, or bloating and sustained you throughout the morning, these foods are in all likelihood fine for you. If you had pasta with meat sauce and a beer for dinner, and you felt uncomfortably full or bloated with gas and then later had a soft stool or diarrhea, there is a good chance you may have a sensitivity to wheat. Once you have done this for a week or two, you will begin to see a pattern that will help determine the foods that are negatively affecting you.

If you find that you are consistently reacting to a specific food, find a practitioner who can help you determine if you are having food sensitivities or a digestive issue. It may be as simple as needing to add digestive enzymes or eliminating certain foods to negate the effects, but you have to go through the discovery process first.

I have had number of patients come in and tell me they cut wheat out of their diets and were frustrated because it didn't have any effect. When questioning them about what effect they wanted, invariably I am told they cut out wheat to lose weight, because it worked for their friend. There is a significant correlation between food sensitivities and an inability to lose weight. It is highly likely that their friend had wheat sensitivity, and they did not. You have to determine specifically what foods, if any, are issues for you.

Bridget was one of those patients who initially came to see me because I had helped her friend deal with a wheat allergy. Her friend suffered from skin rashes and excessive bloating. We removed all wheat/gluten products from her diet, and in about two months, her symptoms were gone and she had lost some weight as well. Bridget had consistent bloating and gas and decided to remove wheat from her diet but this had no effect on her symptoms at all. She opted against doing a blood-work profile to assess if food was a culprit due to the cost, so I suggested that she do a diet diary to help assess what, if any, foods she might be reactive to.

For about two weeks, she dutifully wrote down her foods and how she felt after eating. Every morning, she would get up while her family was still asleep, make herself a latte, and sit down to check and answer emails. When she finished her coffee, she would meditate for fifteen or twenty minutes. She had never noticed before that each time she began to meditate, she would get stuffy and her nose would run. She thought, "I wonder if I have an issue with dairy." Bridget also had a passion for ice cream, which she consumed several days a week. As you might have guessed by now, the ice cream gave her bad gas and uncomfortable bloating. When she reviewed her diet diary, the pattern became very clear that she was indeed reacting to dairy. She removed the dairy from her diet and took probiotics and digestive enzymes, and in about three months, her symptoms were gone.

Discovering if you are sensitive to foods isn't always as simple as it was in the examples of the two patients above. Sometimes you may have symptoms hours or a day later, and it's difficult to put the cause and effect together. Additionally, it is not uncommon for someone to be sensitive to more than one food at a time, which further complicates the issue.

For the most accurate results, I generally recommend blood testin. In our office, we use a company called ALCAT. Using this method allows you to test how reactive you are to foods based on the amount of immunoglobulin reactivity. Food reactions are categorized as severe, moderate, mild, or no reactivity at all. Although each patient is different, I generally recommend that for the severe and moderate food reactivity, they discontinue the foods for a period of six months. After that, we gradually reintroduce them on a rotational basis to determine whether they are able to tolerate the offending foods.

Sugar: Reggie is an eight-year-old boy who is a very picky eater. He started every morning with a heaping bowl of his favorite sugary cereal with milk and a glass of orange juice. Desperate to get him to eat anything, his mom bargained with him that she would let him have a Pop Tart if he ate the cereal and drank his juice first. What eight-year-old wouldn't take that opportunity?

After a few weeks his teacher contacted his mom to inquire about his sleeping habits because he was falling asleep in the middle of the morning and having difficulty staying focused. His mom was puzzled and assured the teacher that he was an excellent sleeper, which was indeed true. When the behavior persisted, she took him to the pediatrician to determine a possible cause. As he took the history regarding play, sleep and social activities, nothing seemed out of balance until they explored his dietary habits.

When she described his typical breakfast, it became immediately apparent that the problem was the result of the high dose of sugar in the cereal, juice, and Pop Tart followed by the crashing low blood sugar levels about two hours later. He explained to Reggie why this was happening to his body and assured him that making changes would keep him out of trouble with his teacher. He advised his mother to replace the cereal with eggs, cheese, and some fruit. He asked her to consider making shapes out of the fruit and cooking his eggs in a mold to make it more appealing. The protein has a longer staying power than the quick-burning carbohydrates and sugar, and this solved the problem almost immediately. Reggie's story is not that uncommon. The amount of sugar that our kids eat is staggering, and it affects their health, concentration, focus and ability to learn as well.

Is sugar really this bad for you? Yep, it is. That doesn't mean that you should never eat sugar, but minimizing the amount and paying attention to the type of sugar you eat is critical.

We are a nation that overindulges in all kinds of sugary and processed foods. Diabetes is out of control in this country, and the statistics get worse every day. Walking down the cereal aisle in your grocery store or going into a gas station mini-store are prime examples of the excessive variety of sugar options we have available. Have you ever noticed all the sugar products available in the checkout line? It is no accident that they are placed there for us to stare at while we wait our turn to checkout. Billions of dollars are spent annually to monitor behavior and develop better ways of enticing us to consume.

As parents, we are the gatekeepers for the foods our children eat, and therefore, we have a responsibility to teach them how to eat properly. It can be a tough job considering the barrage of advertisements they see, not to mention the toys or rewards they receive when purchasing fast foods or cereals. It is also difficult if you yourself have never been educated about food.

Sugar not only affects the quality of your day but can also be a significant factor in your child's success or failure in school. Consumption of refined, sugary foods will cause a release of insulin from your pancreas, which rapidly delivers sugar to your brain and muscles, giving you a burst of energy. Unfortunately, when you have a sugar-handling problem and sugar enters your bloodstream it causes a spike in the blood sugar immediately followed by low blood sugar, resulting in fatigue, irritability, headache, difficulty concentrating, depression, and even hyperactivity.

This roller coaster of energy makes it difficult to stay focused to learn or get work done. It's not just the kids who get affected by the ups and downs of the sugar roller coaster. It is all of us. Often we develop these habits as children, which, if left unchallenged, continue throughout our adult life.

Know your foods: In order to eat a balanced diet, you have to understand what food category your food falls into. Is your food a fat, protein, or carbohydrate? This is confusing to many people. What would you say if I asked you what category an orange or apple belongs in? If you are like most of my patients, you probably thought it was a fruit or vegetable, both of which are not categories at all. An orange is a carbohydrate, as are most all fruits.

Knowing what a whole grain is versus a refined grain is extremely important when choosing to eat any grain. A whole grain, when subjected to a high-heat milling process that removes the germ and bran, is left with only the starch, which makes it a refined grain. The starch in the refined grain contains primarily sugar. Unfortunately, it also removes many of the nutrients, such as vitamin E, which are critical to good health.

Kim is a very conscientious mom and always goes the extra mile to make sure her kids are eating healthy snacks. One day, she came in with her son Ben, who was inhaling a sandwich while he was waiting for his mother. "What are you eating, Ben?" I casually asked.

He responded with, "turkey, avocado, and sprouts." Kim quickly added, "On a really good whole wheat bread."

"What makes it so good"? I asked.

"It's fortified and enriched, so it's much better than regular white bread." she said.

I explained to her that the only reason it is fortified and enriched is because they take out all the nutrients when they do the processing, and then they have to put it back in to meet industry standards. Instead of telling you that side of the story, they make it into a marketing issue so that you think you are getting something much better, which you are not. If you have to eat bread, get it from a local bakery that uses fresh ingredients. It not only tastes better, it is better for you.

Try replacing refined grains with oat, barley, brown rice, or millet flours, all of which have a great taste and can easily be substituted in most recipes. Carbohydrates such as bread and pasta are made of sugar molecules and, when broken down, are not that much different than regular sugar. Interestingly, refined wheat flour has so little nutrition in it that farmers report that even bugs living in the silo can't sustain themselves on it.

Fruits and vegetables are loaded with vitamins and minerals, and, with some exceptions, are usually lower in calories. It is recommended that at least half of your plate should be filled with fruits and vegetables with each meal. Fruits are also a great way to satisfy a sweet tooth. Many fruits and vegetables contain fiber, which bind with toxins in your colon to allow for proper bowel function.

High fiber foods such as beans, legumes, raw fruits, vegetables, and whole grains are essential to proper colon function. Proper colon function is significant in maintaining your weight and ridding your body of toxins. It is virtually impossible to live in a healthy body without the ability to rid yourself of the daily influx of toxins that we take in. These toxins don't just come from the foods we eat either. It is also the pollution in our air, as well as toxins in our medications, hair products, lotions, and creams. All of these things enter our system on a daily basis and must be removed in order for us to maintain a healthy body. Having good colon function, ample urine output, and sweating are critical in order for that to happen. Being conscious of how and what you fill your plate with dramatically increases your chance of maintaining your weight and living in a healthy body.

Pamela is a forty-five-year-old flight attendant who came in for a nutritional consult. She was about fifteen pounds overweight and told me that no matter what she did, she could not lose more than a pound or two. Her health history was fairly unremarkable with one exception. She only had a bowel movement about every third or fourth day. She had been eating mostly protein to lose weight, and her diet consisted of very few fruits or vegetables. She didn't like to drink anything because she felt it made her gain water-weight.

I explained to her that your body needs a good amount of water each day to help rid it of the toxins that are produced as waste. When you don't drink enough water, your body will take water from the colon, leaving your fecal material drier, and you can end up constipated. In addition to that, your colon needs fiber to form a good stool and the protein she was eating contained very little fiber.

I put her on a balanced diet containing fruits, vegetables, and good fats and increased her water intake one hundred percent. She was reluctant at first, but when I saw her again three weeks later, she had lost seven pounds and was having daily bowel movements. Often, feeling better is just getting the balance right.

Eat organic: Whenever possible eat foods that are grown organically. Yes, sometimes you have to pay a little more, but in the long run, it is totally worth minimizing the consumption of large amounts of pesticides commonly used in commercially grown food. Many of our foods have been genetically modified, and little by little, the results are showing that this is having more negative effects on people than they thought it would. Modifying the genes of these plants have increased the yield of the plant, increased its ability to resist pests, and made them more resilient and resistant to disease. Unfortunately, it has changed so much that the immune system of many people no longer recognize it and attack it as a foreign invader. Likewise, our milk is often radiated and contains a statement on the side of the carton that states that "No significant difference has been shown in milk from cows treated with the artificial growth hormone rbST and non-rbST treated cows." Doesn't it make you wonder why they are required to put that on the carton? It's easy to avoid giving our kids this growth hormone by just buying organic.

One possibility to consider is a food co-op. This is a system where a number of people get together, pool their money, and pay a farmer a certain amount of money each month. In return, they get a delivery of fresh vegetables each week based on whatever is in season. It is generally very economical since you have cut out the middleman and is considerably fresher than what you would get in the store.

Avoid or limit fruit juices: Fruit juices are loaded with sugar, which is one of the reasons they taste so good. Many people drink orange or grapefruit juice everyday with the wholehearted belief that they are enriching their bodies with a good dose of vitamin C. The problem is, that in addition to the vitamin C, a typical eight-ounce glass of orange juice is loaded with twenty-one grams of sugar, which is three more grams than a piece of apple pie!

Consider realistic portion sizes: The caloric needs vary from person to person and, therefore, so do the portion sizes. The caloric needs of a twenty-year-old active male versus a fifty-year-old fairly sedentary female vary widely. For example, a twenty-year-old male may consume 2500 to three thousand calories a day and still maintain a good weight whereas a fifty-year-old female may need to stay under 1500 calories to maintain her weight. Consider eating four to five smaller meals throughout the day. When we allow for long spans of time in between our meals, our blood sugar may drop too low, and when we do finally eat, we are ravenous and tend to over eat. Eating small meals throughout the day totally avoids the overconsumption of calories. This will help to keep your blood sugar stable and to avoid energy highs and lows. Realistically, if you are maintaining a comfortable weight, you are probably eating the correct portion sizes. If you are gaining weight, especially a little at a time, there is a good chance you are eating portion sizes that are too large for your frame.

Avoid fast food: According to an article in the Huffington Post, there were 263,944 fast food restaurants in America with combined revenue of over one hundred billion dollars in 2012 (Jacques 2013)! A Gallop poll also revealed that eight in ten Americans eat fast food. If you ever took the time to research what was in these foods and how they were made, I can promise you that you would think twice before sidling up to the window. These companies spend millions of dollars in advertising to entice you to eat their food; in addition, they offer your children toys and gifts so they can pressure you to go there too.

Most fast foods contain high caloric, fat, and sodium content, all of which contribute to a wide variety of health issues. In addition to the high caloric value, many fast foods are also high in saturated fats, which are a risk factor in heart disease. A regular meal at McDonald's with a Big Mac, French fries, and a large Coke amounts to a whopping 1,430 calories, and that's just one meal. For some, that is their entire calorie allotment for the day.

To assist you in regulating yourself, I encourage you to consider using an inexpensive app such as "Lose It" to monitor your calories consumed and burned. There are also more sophisticated, expensive wrist devices, such as Jawbone or Fitbit, that will sync with your computer or smartphone to relay all kinds of information, such as calories burned, how well you sleep, heart rate, and much more. Awareness is the key to success for staying healthy, and these devices allow you to input significant data that can keep you on track.

How you feel everyday plays a significant role in whether you are living in your sweet spot or not. Food affects how you feel, and how you feel affects how you live your life. Take the time to assess how the foods you consume are contributing to the success or failure of living the life you want to live. You are totally in charge of what and how much you put in your mouth. Taking the time to be mindful of what you buy, make, and consume will go a long way in helping you to live a healthy and happy life. It's not that difficult to choose fruits, vegetables, and whole grains over sugars, but we often let our emotions and taste buds take charge. The good news is that we get an opportunity several times a day to make these choices. The more that we make the correct choices the more habitual it becomes. Take the time to make good choices and develop good eating habits for yourself. You will not be disappointed.

Chapter 12

Sleep

S leep is our most precious and often most overlooked gift. One of the questions I ask when I am doing nutritional consults is how long and how well do you sleep? The reason for this is how you sleep plays a significant role in how healthy and happy you are.

We are more tired as a nation and as individuals than we were in previous centuries. This does not bode well for living in your sweet spot or being your authentic self. The problem is that sleep deprivation is generally chronic in nature and often goes unnoticed by many because it becomes their norm. The fact that a cup of coffee may be needed to get the day started is often never given a second thought. I often hear people express, "I just don't sleep well," as if that was that and it wasn't going to change. It can change and needs to in order for you to live well.

Statistics show that poor sleep plays a role in virtually every aspect of disease and disease-related issues, as well as your ability to perform your everyday activities of daily living and diminishes your performance on the playing field. Despite various mandates given on the amount of sleep that you need, each of us has our own unique sleep requirement, which varies by age, sex, and genetic and physiological factors. A good rule of thumb, however, is that a sufficient amount of sleep is that which allows for spontaneous awakening and leaves you with enough energy to feel refreshed and alert for the whole day. One of the ways that I will find out if my patients have had enough sleep is to ask them, "When you are done at the end of the day, do you have enough energy to go out and do something else if you wanted to"? Frequently, the answer is, "If I really wanted to or had to, I can usually get it together to go out" instead of "absolutely" or "sure."

Studies have shown that we are getting less and less sleep as time has gone on. Between 1959 and 1992, we went from eight or nine hours per night to seven or eight hours per night. A recent study by the National Institutes of Health found we now get an average of six hours of sleep per night. It is reported that this has more to do with external factors, such as having to work two jobs, single parenting requiring more time in a day to get things done, having to work longer shifts, and, in general, more time consumed by multimedia than it does with biological factors.

There are many reasons why people don't sleep well, and with systematic evaluation, the root cause can be uncovered and frequently resolved. Causes such as breathing issues, adrenal fatigue, drinking too much alcohol too late, shift work, worrying, hormonal changes, sleeping environments, and even animals in your bed all play a role in how well you do or do not sleep.

According to leading sleep researchers, these are the top ten questions to ask yourself when trying to correct sleeping problems. How does your sleeping rate?

1. Do you keep a regular sleep-wake cycle?

2. Are you drinking or eating caffeine for up to six hours before bedtime, and are you mindful of your daytime consumption?

3. Do you avoid smoking near bedtime or if you awaken in the night?

4. Do you avoid alcohol and heavy meals later in the evening?

5. Do you get regular exercise?

6. Have you minimized noise, light, and excessive hot or cold temperatures where you sleep?

7. Do you go to bed at the same time each night?

8. Can you awaken without an alarm clock?

9. Do you sleep with animals in your bed?

10. Do you have a successful method for dealing with excessive thoughts or worry while trying to go to sleep?

Let's discuss in more detail how each of these factors can become an issue and some possible solutions for each.

Breathing: One possible scenario is that it may be a breathing problem. Sleep apnea is a condition in which you temporarily stop breathing while sleeping. It's more common than you may think, and it causes an individual to wake up frequently throughout the night. This results in waking up groggy, sleepy, not at all rested, and usually tired throughout the day. The individual affected is sometimes not even aware of how often they are awakening or that their breathing is affected at all. Frequently, the person that they sleep with reports the irregularity in their breath and snoring. The snoring will stop for a short period of time, such as a few seconds, and then abruptly the individual will produce a sound that sounds like a gasp, followed by the resumption of the snoring.

This turned out to be the case for one of my patients. Joan came in one day, and in the course of conversation, I mentioned that she looked tired.

"I am dog-tired," she replied. I am having a really hard time sleeping with Bob's snoring, and it is keeping me up all through the night. I will just start to fall back asleep and then he starts in again. Can't you do something about that?" she joked.

Bob is also a patient and has never mentioned sleep issues, fatigue, or anything related, despite my having questioned him directly. I questioned Joan a little further.

"Does he snore every night?"

"Absolutely, like clockwork," she replied. "He starts snoring, and then, every few minutes, I think, it stops. Then he takes a big breath and starts in again. It's maddening."

I knew immediately from her description that Bob probably had sleep apnea. The pause that she was describing happens when his breathing has stopped, and the big breath was the way his body was dealing with oxygen deficiency.

"Does it get real quiet when the snoring stops" I asked her.

"Yes, real quiet, and I am real grateful."

I suggested she have Bob come into see me so we could determine what we could do about his snoring.

"He and I have never talked about his snoring," I remarked.

"Oh," she exclaimed. "I am sure that's true. He denies he even snores!"

Bob did come in (and denied he snores) but I explained what I thought might be happening and sent him off for a sleep study. Diagnosis is simple and involves having your breathing assessed while you sleep through the night. If you are diagnosed with sleep apnea, you will, in all likelihood, be prescribed a CPAP machine that you wear at night, which regulates your breathing and ensures that you get enough oxygen through the night. The results can and often do make an incredibly significant difference. People report feeling more refreshed, having more energy, getting sick less often and many report weight loss. This often occurs when people start to sleep better, and there is good research that supports the association between sufficient sleep and weight loss.

Needless to say, Bob was prescribed and now uses a CPAP machine. He has stopped snoring and is feeling much more rested and energetic. His wife is a lot happier and well rested too. An additional side benefit that occurred was that Bob also began to lose weight, which he had struggled with for years.

Adrenal fatigue: Another factor that can contribute to poor sleep is adrenal fatigue. The adrenals are two small glands that sit on top of the kidneys and are responsible for many functions in the body, especially responding to stress. They release what we call the "flight or fight" hormones. When we are faced with a stressful moment, we will either run from it or stay and fight. Either way is stressful. Once the stressful event has passed, the adrenals stop the flood of adrenaline and return to a resting state. Unfortunately, many of us live stressful lives and our adrenal glands don't get a lot of down time. We are a more "pedal to the metal" kind of society, and rest for the sake of rest is often overlooked.

I'm certain at some point you have heard people make comments such as, "I wasted a whole morning reading a book" or "we wasted the day just hanging out." I can't help but wonder what is the waste in that. Unfortunately, somehow we have gotten to the place in our society where not being productive is wasting time. My belief is that downtime is the place where dreams and ideas are born. Some of my greatest insights have come from lying at the beach being completely lazy or sitting at the dog park mindlessly watching the dogs play. Creating this kind of time on a regular basis is important on many levels.

When the adrenal glands get fatigued from a lack of downtime, they begin to function less optimally. I am not referring to the extremes of Addison's or Cushing's disease, where we have way too much or too little adrenal function. I am referring to functional adrenal issues where the adrenal glands are fatigued, not diseased.

The adrenal glands do more than just pump out adrenaline when we get under stress. They have control over a whole host of other hormones. One hormone that the adrenal controls is cortisol. You may have heard about cortisol on TV and in ads that deal with how to rid yourself of belly fat. While it is true that improper cortisol levels do play a role in belly fat, they also play a large role in your sleep. When the adrenals begin to fatigue, one of the first things that gets out of balance is the cortisol rhythm. They should rise and fall in a specific pattern throughout the day. If your cortisol levels are out of balance, falling asleep is difficult.

Proper cortisol levels also help to keep your blood glucose levels steady throughout the day. When you have low cortisol levels, your blood sugar level drops, which leaves you feeling tired. One of the first things people often do is reach for the caffeinated or sugary beverages, which cause the blood sugar levels to rise rapidly then crash again, making the cycle worse and further stressing the adrenal glands.

If you are waking up between one and three in the morning, your liver may be lacking the glycogen reserves needed by the adrenals to keep blood glucose levels high enough through the night. Glucose is what your brain eats, and it is stored in the liver in the form of glycogen. Even though blood glucose levels are generally low in the morning, if you suffer from adrenal fatigue, these levels may drop low enough in the night to cause hypoglycemic (low blood sugar) symptoms that will wake you up.

Counteracting the low blood sugar is easily remedied by eating a small snack before bed, such as peanut butter on a cracker or a piece of cheese on a cracker. Both of these snacks have protein and high quality fat for sustainability, as well as refined carbohydrate to raise the blood sugar levels. Even though this specific problem can be remedied by having a snack, it is extremely important that the issue of the adrenal fatigue be addressed as well. The waking is indicative of the larger issue of adrenal fatigue, not just the fact that your brain is hungry. The snack will definitely help your sleep issues in the short run, but to be well and live in your sweet spot, the adrenal fatigue must be addressed and healed.

One way to assist the adrenals in healing is to decrease the level of sugar in your diet and get an adequate amount of protein. Protein causes your blood sugar levels to stay on an even keel, whereas carbo-hydrates and sugar cause an endless cycle of rising and falling sugar levels. Caffeine also causes your adrenals to overreact, stressing the adrenals, and should be avoided as much as possible.

Michael is a thirty-nine-year-old male, married with two children, one of whom is special needs. He started a catering business about three years ago, which has become highly successful. He is at the stage where he is pushing to the next level and needs to hire more people. He has been hesitant because he is afraid the additional workers will strain him financially. As a result, he is working long hours, many of which go late into the evening since catering frequently is a nighttime activity. He is seeing less of his family and friends, having no fun, and enduring more stress, all because he truly believes this is the best way to support his family and create a successful business.

He came in to see me because he was feeling achy with low back pain and having difficulty sleeping. Michael is great guy, and I always enjoy talking with him. In the course of conversation, I asked what was happening with his sleep. He related that his sleep was suffering because he could get to sleep, but he then would awaken around two in the morning and couldn't get his brain to shut off.

"Silly things," he said. "I lie and there and think of things like how much butter will they need or did I order enough chicken? All the while, I know that I have enough and have ordered correctly. Then I start thinking about Nancy and how I never get to see her anymore. She's usually in bed when I get home, and we haven't made love in months. To tell you the truth, I don't think the thing works anymore."

I asked him if he was having difficulty sustaining an erection.

"Yes," Michael responded. "I just think I am too tired."

I explained to him that the fatigue may be partly to blame, but it was not the only reason. The adrenal glands may be a factor in not only his fatigue but his erection difficulty as well. Long-term stress can have an impact on the adrenals and their function, and it was my suspicion that this was the case for him.

A saliva study is one of the most effective ways to determine how the adrenals are functioning when not in an extreme response. Blood-level studies are the most effective when we are dealing with the extremes of over-and-under-functioning adrenals, such as in the case of Addison's or Cushing's diseases.

We ran a salivary study on Michael's adrenals, and found that, indeed, his adrenals were functioning at a very low level and his cortisol rhythms were significantly out of balance. Additionally, his DHEA was low. This was significant because DHEA is a precursor for testosterone production, which helped account for some of his lack of sex drive and the inability to get or maintain an erection.

Once we reviewed the test results, he was excited and willing to do what it took to feel better. Initially, Michael had wanted me to give him something to take but I explained that there was a lot more to it than just taking a supplement. It takes time to develop this problem, and it won't go away overnight. In general, it takes about a year or so for the adrenals to fully heal. This involves not only supporting the adrenals with supplements but also addressing the initiating behaviors that created the problem.

I explained that this involved getting some help at work, which meant he probably would have to let go of trying to control everything, spread some of the responsibilities around, and trust the people he had hired to do the work he had given them. I suggested he start going home earlier a few days a week, relax more, and get adequate rest. The five or six hours a night that he had been getting just wouldn't be enough to allow for healing. I also suggested he get out and exercise so he could get some vitamin D.

I reminded him of when he used to play racquetball every week with his buddies.

"You haven't done that in as long as I can remember."

"It's true," he said. "I miss those guys."

I suggested that he slowly make his way back to an aggressive activity such as racquetball. However, racquetball is a rigorous sport, so it was important for Michael not to over exercise with adrenal fatigue. Over-exercising will create additional stress on the adrenals and further fatigue you, but moderate exercise will help, so I asked him to start with brisk walks and suggested he take Nancy with him when possible to get some alone time with her.

Modifying the things that created the stress on the adrenal gland is critical for successful healing. Michael needed to prioritize what was truly important and make decisions based on trust and not out of fear. The things that aren't important either need to be let go of or given to someone else to do.

There are effective supplements that can be of value in helping the adrenals to heal fully. I gave him liquid licorice root as a supplement, which helps to mimic the effects of cortisol, as well as Siberian ginseng, which is related to a precursor of DHEA, and cortisol. Additionally, I asked him to monitor his blood pressure outside of the office because in some individuals, licorice root can increase their blood pressure, and it is important to monitor its effects and make changes if necessary. Additionally, I asked him to give up the five to six cups of coffee he drank daily. He negotiated hard for his coffee, so we settled on one cup a day or green tea.

Michael was motivated, and, in about six months' time, he was feeling significantly better. He had had to make some hard decisions, most of which involved letting go of trying to control everything. He was spending three nights a week at home and enjoying more loving and intimate time with his wife and family. He was also getting out with his buddies every two weeks or so. His erection issues were resolved, he is sleeping well, and he is finally enjoying his life and business again.

This may sound like a simple story with a happy ending, but I can't emphasize enough that it wasn't simple for Michael and it isn't simple for most people. He had to face some hard truths and fears, and only by putting all the pieces together did he begin the process of healing his adrenals and getting his life back on track.

Hormones: Estrogen and progesterone are two primary hormones that affect sleep. This occurs during all phases of menopause, including peri- or post-menopauses. Decreasing estrogen levels causes women to have difficulty staying asleep and minimizes the amount of time spent in REM sleep. REM sleep helps the brain make sense of the day's events through dreaming, refreshing the mind, and leaving you with a clean slate in the morning. Progesterone, on the other hand, affects the part of the brain that causes you to feel sleepy. As these hormone levels drop, women often have trouble falling asleep. In a recent study, it was determined that women with low estrogen awake three to five times more at night than those with normal estrogen levels (Murck et al. 2006).

The decreased estrogen also fosters hot flashes, which unfortunately often occur at night. As the hot flashes occur, women tend to awaken frequently and throw the covers off to relieve the internal inferno, followed by being cold and searching the bed to get back under the covers. This disruptive sleep-wake cycle often leaves women fatigued upon awakening and affects the entire day. The frequency of this varies from woman to woman, but it is disruptive to all, no matter how frequent.

Husbands and partners are often impacted by this sleep cycle as well because women are often anything but subtle when these hot flashes occur, and their thrashing about often wakes their sleep mates. A woman will generally awaken just before the hot flash occurs and then stay awake until she is able to fall back asleep, which is difficult due to the low levels of progesterone.

There are many options to assist you in dealing with the hot flashes and hormonal changes. What to do is always a personal choice and should be based on your own medical history, as well as your family history. If the sleep disruption is affecting your quality of life, estrogen replacement therapy is an option for some. Recent research shows that it may be safe for women in their fifties to take the new lower doses if used for less than five years. Additionally, some natural alternatives have been shown to reduce hot flashes, such as black cohosh, wild yam, chaste tree, and others.

Personally, I come with a family history of breast cancer and estrogen therapy is not a risk I was willing to undertake or consider. I have found acupuncture to be an incredibly effective tool for my hot flashes. I get treated about once a month, and this procedure has essentially eradicated the hot flashes completely. I sleep much better, and there are no side effects. If your sleep is disrupted from hormonal changes, talk with your doctor and discuss what your best options are based on your medical history and personal preferences.

Estrogen and progesterone aren't the only hormones that have an effect on our sleep. Melatonin is one of these hormones, which is produced by the pineal gland and unfortunately decreases with age. Melatonin, when released, causes us to feel drowsy as darkness occurs. Low levels of melatonin also create difficulty in falling asleep. If you find this is an issue for you, talk with your physician about possibly supplementing your diet with melatonin. If low melatonin is the underlying cause, using the supplement can prove to be very effective.

Alcohol and food: Many people use alcohol as their sedative to induce sleep. While it is true that alcohol may reduce the amount of time it takes to get to sleep, alcohol consumed close to bedtime has been shown to disrupt the second half of the sleep cycle. Studies show that even moderate amounts of alcohol consumed later in the day, such as during "happy hour" or with dinner or as much as six hours before bedtime, can increase wakefulness during the second sleep cycle phase. Generally, late-night nippers will have a tendency to sleep fitfully, have dreams that awaken them, and have difficulty returning to sleep. Studies show that long-term alcohol abuse may provoke severe insomnia. Most do not realize that alcohol's effect on the brain is two to three times greater at midnight, which is one cause of nighttime mortality. The later you consume alcohol, the greater the effect on your system.

Eating and drinking late or too close to bedtime can also cause heartburn and/or acid reflux, which disrupts sleep as acid backs up into the esophagus. If you have to eat late for whatever reason, eat on the lighter side to avoid indigestion and disruption of your sleep patterns, and consider eating a larger meal earlier in the day.

Conversely, going to bed hungry can also cause you to awaken due to low-blood sugar. Many a dieter will choose to avoid eating anything or eating very little for the evening meal, believing that they are conserving the calories when, in fact, it does just the opposite. Not only are you awakened due to low blood sugar, but eating very little also slows down your metabolism and you burn fewer calories! This ends up as a lose-lose situation. You lose precious sleep, don't burn as many calories, and you are hungry.

Saving some of your calories for a high protein snack, such as cheese or a hardboiled egg, close to bedtime will eliminate the possibility of hypoglycemia and make it more likely that you will lose more weight. It has always been hard for people to get the concept that you have to eat to lose weight. Those of you who have been on the famed Weight Watchers plan successfully know that the point value system that they use is important, not only because it limits how much you can eat, but also because it tells you how much you have to eat. Both eating too much or too little will prevent you from losing the weight you want to lose.

Worrying: Worrying about your relationship, money, job, any big changes—marriage, buying a house, or starting a new job—or even worrying about your sleep itself can all cause you not to sleep well. There is a condition known as "psychological insomnia," and it happens when you worry about your sleep so much that it becomes a job. Your mind reviews over and over what you have to do the next day, and then you worry that you aren't going to get enough sleep, which, of course, you don't. Finding ways to turn your brain off and control the runaway thoughts is essential to getting the rest you need.

For some, writing lists before the end of the day helps to organize their thoughts, which then lets their brains take a rest. For others, it is a matter of doing something calming—taking a bath or meditating—to redirect their minds. Some read and others watch TV. Personally, I have done all of these. My favorite way to stop my brain is that, just after I lie down, I visualize the thing or things that are worrying me, mentally place them in an imaginary box, and mentally place the box beside the bed, trusting that everything I need to deal with will be there in the morning. Somehow, actively removing these things from my brain and theoretically putting them somewhere else works well for me.

Recently, we made the transition in our office to electronic medical records, which was a major undertaking and changed virtually every aspect of how the office functioned. It affected how patients sign in, records are recorded, how payments are made, and how insurance is processed. Even though the transition went smoothly, it was not without many restless nights of sleep for all of us in the office. I would lie in bed thinking of every possible scenario that might go wrong in the hope of averting it before it happened.

It wasn't until I was incredibly fatigued and irritable that I had to stop and remember, "Oh yeah, I can do something about this!" This scenario brings up an important point: even though I talk about this every day to my patients and in every workshop I teach, I still can have an occasional moment where I forget to take care of myself. For many, the first thing to go when they get stressed is sleeping, working out, or eating well. The important thing is not to judge it but to get back on track as soon as you recognize what has happened. It takes dedication and mindful behavior to get in the habit of staying on track when you are under stress. Most of us have a tendency to revert to old, comfy habits when under stress, but if you have found what works for and you choose that first when you are under stress instead of the TV, alcohol, or couch, you are going to be much more successful in your self-care.

Money is another issue that affects many individuals' ability to sleep peacefully. Do I have enough, where am I going to get it, and will I have it in time are questions often running through people's minds as they try to go to sleep. Money isn't everything, but it sure does pay for a lot and gives us lots of options. When money is scarce, it's understandable why people get concerned, but worrying doesn't solve this issue and generally leaves you in a negative mindset that affects other areas of your life.

When worrying interferes with your sleep, it leaves you more fatigued, generally with a shorter fuse, and less likely to come up with possible solutions. Try some of the options I mentioned earlier to help get you to sleep. In addition, I find gratitude is particularly effective for shifting a worrisome negative mental state. If your money stress leaves you with troublesome thoughts, coming up with what you are grateful for can be helpful. Start simple with things such as being grateful you have running water, a toilet, a bed to sleep in, no bombs in your yard, or the freedom to make your own decisions. It will definitely start to put things in perspective.

Animals: Many sleep issues, as well as back pain, have been simply resolved by getting our beloved pets out of the bed. Don't get me wrong: I love my dog, and she is the best snuggler in the world, but if I let her, she would have the whole king-sized bed to herself before morning. Admittedly, more than half of dog and cat owners sleep with their beloved pets. Whether it is dog, cat, or whatever, my experience is that people report they will constantly change their positions to accommodate their animals, sacrificing their own comfort and disrupting their sleep.

On a recent visit, Laura came in with mid-back pain and spasms that started a few days prior when the dog she was walking fell in love with a squirrel that she just had to have. The dog took off running and pulled her halfway down the block before she could get it under control. Laura and Barry have two large, beautiful blonde Labrador retrievers that they adore. After I had taken care of the injury, I asked if her pain was disrupting her sleep.

"Not the pain," she answered. "Just the dogs. We have a queen-sized bed, and when Barry and I wake up in the morning, we are clinging to the edges of the bed and the dogs are the ones sleeping like queens. We're clinging to the sides of the bed, and they sleep back-to-back with their legs straight out. We never sleep well unless we're on vacation and have left the dogs at home."

"I know you probably aren't going to like this, but in order for you to get well, you are going to have to get the dogs out of the bed," I said.

"I'll just sleep in the other room until it's better," she responded.

"I didn't say better, I said well. There is no way you are going to be well until you start sleeping, and you are not going to sleep well until you have your space back. Not to mention, you'll probably enjoy sleeping next to your husband again."

I asked her to retrain them to sleep next to her, beside the bed. Putting down some blankets and old t-shirts with her and her husband's smell on them made the transition easier. Their dogs were fairly resistant, but in two weeks or so, Laura and Barry had them sleeping on the floor, and, finally, were sleeping through the night and waking up rested.

This is an all too common issue. Many people sleep with their pets and this can significantly impact their sleep cycles. Our animals snore, wake up during the night, get water, and walk around just like humans, all of which can disrupt our sleep. Consider whether this may be a problem for you, and if so, devise a plan for getting them out of the bed and preferably out of your room.

Sleep environment: Light in your bedroom can easily disrupt your sleep. Get rid of or cover ambient light, such as alarm clocks, DVD players, or cable boxes. Using room-darkening curtains and shades can significantly enhance your ability to sleep deeply. Even a small amount of brightness can trigger your retina even when your eyes are closed. The light sends a signal to your brain and upsets your sleep-wake cycle, which results in making you feel more awake. Minimize light leaks, and if this is not possible, consider wearing a soft, comfortable sleep mask to block the light. This allows for deeper sleep and more time in REM sleep.

Temperature is also a consideration. Sleeping in a room that is too hot or too cold will disrupt the deepness of your sleep. Set your temperature gauge to a comfortable setting, preferably on the cooler side, and adjust your bed linens accordingly.

As you can see, many factors can affect your sleep. Getting adequate sleep is extremely important, not only for living your authentic life, but also for being able to enjoy living it. Everything from how much light there is in your bedroom, to what and how you eat, to how your hormones are impacting you. Evaluate your quality of sleep from all perspectives, and if you make the adjustments where necessary, you will likely find yourself being more restful and present while enjoying your life to the fullest. With a systematic approach, you can uncover what issues are significant for you and hopefully begin to enjoy deep, peaceful sleep.

Chapter 13

Exercise

Maryanne came in one day for a follow-up visit for a shoulder injury that she had developed while throwing pots. No, she wasn't actually throwing pots. She had taken up making pottery as a hobby when she retired.

She's in her midsixties and really enjoying her retirement, but her body had started to take a beating with minor injuries coming to the surface. While we were discussing whether or not she has been doing the rehab exercises I had given her, she began talking about how she really wished she had gotten the Cliffs Notes on aging.

Sensing an opportunity, I asked, "What do you mean by that?"

"Well, if I'd have known that I was going to lose all this muscle mass and be so wimpy, I would have paid more attention and done more to keep myself in shape."

For most individuals, our muscle strength will reach its maximal contractual capacity and strength somewhere around age twenty and then begin to decrease. Strength training is particularly important as we age. It is even more important for woman than men. Men have a higher level of testosterone, which makes muscle development easier. Women have higher levels of estrogen, which makes it harder to build muscle strength. Muscle strength also becomes significant as we age because weakness is associated with balance issues, which have been shown to correlate with falls and increase injury and mortality.

"Well, it's not too late, and I actually have the Cliffs Notes," I responded with a smile.

"I hate exercise!" She quickly and loudly exclaimed.

"Do you really hate exercise or do you not do the things that you like to do?"

I asked this because I find that many people either avoid doing the things they love, because they think it doesn't count as exercise, or they have not or are unwilling to try the things that do interest them.

The most recent statistics gathered by the CDC as to why people don't exercise indicate that 38% have no time, 37% say it's too much trouble, 12% don't like it, 4% can't afford it, and 9% have some other reason but they don't know what that is. Exercise doesn't always have to be lifting weights and running on a treadmill or elliptical. It's about getting yourself moving in whatever way works for you.

Walk, do yoga, get a Wii Fit and play games, ride a bike, go for a hike, play golf, or throw a Frisbee with a friend. It doesn't matter what it is. What matters is that you do it. Although it is changing somewhat as we age, more people have a tendency to do less exercise. This is the worst time for that to happen. We have less bone density, an increase in disease, and a high probability of balance issues just around the corner. Simply getting yourself moving and increasing your core strength can dramatically decrease all three.

I pushed Maryanne further, "What do you like to do?"

"I hate going to the gym," she dryly replied, ignoring my question. "It is so boring and I can never keep up in those silly classes. They're going one way and I'm always going the other. I feel like a fool. I had a membership at the Y for a year and went twice. When you work out the math, I think each work out cost me about a hundred bucks."

"I'm not so good at those classes either, but what do you like to do?" I persisted.

"I hate lifting weights too," she said, again avoiding my question entirely. "It's about as exciting as watching paint dry. And, on top of that, you have to listen to those fools grunting."

"I can really see that if I need to find you, the gym is the last place I should look. But what do you like to do?"

"Well, I do like riding bikes. It feels so good to just get on that thing and ride with no particular destination. I like feeling the wind in my hair, checking out the neighborhood, and seeing everyone in his or her yard out and about. I especially like riding at the beach. I ride my brother's bike down there, and I love it because it's so flat and I feel like I can go for days and the air smells so good!"

"Well, that's good exercise," I said. "So how often do you ride?"

"Never," she replied. "I don't have a bike."

"Okay. Here's the first page of the Cliffs Notes. Do what you love. When you leave here today, go to REI or some other bike store and check out the bikes. They always have a huge selection, and the salespeople are generally really helpful. Last time I was in a bike store getting my daughter a new bike, there was a woman just about your age buying a bike, and they had her trying out all different kinds of bikes before she found the one she wanted."

It goes without saying that exercise is extremely valuable, but the way in which it is valuable may just surprise you. After extensive research, it turns out that a moderately fit fat person actually has a lower morbidity rate and is less likely to die of disease than a thin person who is fairly sedentary. This was clearly shown in a longitudinal study performed by Dr. Chi Pang Wen, et al. (2011).

In his book *The Obesity Paradox* (2014), cardiologist Carl J. Lavie, outlines how training for marathons and other extreme sports are actually more damaging to your body than moderate mindful movement. For example, taking a light jog around the park a few times a week is much better for you than training for a marathon, and only forty minutes of exercise four to five times a week is optimal. You can see it really doesn't take much effort to take care of yourself and reduce your mortality rate. Riding your bike or taking a brisk walk with friends or family will all help.

It was also found that, with extreme training, athletes release a substance called troponin, which is the same substance associated with heart attacks and is related to scarring of heart tissue. This is not to say that the levels that are excreted are the same levels as those we find in people who have had a heart attack, but it turns out the accumulated release of the troponin over time adds up and promotes scar tissue around the heart.

For many, intimidation prohibits exercise. I have heard all kinds of reasons: "I don't know how to use the machines," "I don't want anybody to see me like this," "I am afraid to walk in my neighborhood," "I don't know what to buy," "Everybody is so in shape at the gym and I feel out of place," "I don't want to feel stupid," and hundreds more.

I suggested to Maryanne, "You may want to try a bike that has a few more gear options since it's not that flat here, and it's pretty simple to learn. I think if you have an easier time of it, you would be much more likely to ride. It would also be more enjoyable if you didn't have to work so hard. Just consider it and keep all your options open."

Two weeks later Maryanne returned for a follow-up. "Before you ask," she said, "yes, I got a bike, and, yes, I love it!"

"How's the shoulder?"

"Better. I am feeling stronger, and I think getting out on the bike is making me feel like doing other things."

Sensing another opportunity, I prodded Maryanne a little further, "Other things? Like what?"

"Oh, I don't know, maybe a sit up or two."

Her experience is not unusual. According to research conducted by the Mayo Clinic, exercise improves your mood and boosts your energy. Physical activity stimulates various brain chemicals that leave you feeling happier and more relaxed. Once you have begun to exercise, trying different types also becomes less risky. Additionally, it promotes better sleep, puts the spark back into your sex life, and can help to prevent or manage all kinds of health risks, such as heart disease, stroke, diabetes, metabolic syndrome, and depression and many others.

"Can I give you the next page of the Cliffs Notes?"

"You can try," she responded with a smile.

I said to Maryanne, "Well, if you're ready, I want to give you a few exercises to start getting your core muscles strong, which is critically important, not only for keeping your lower back in good shape but also, at your age, it is very helpful for maintaining balance. Many injuries that happen to seniors occur due to falls, and this will help prevent that. They will probably feel awkward at first, but as you continue to do them, you will notice that they only get easier and you will feel stronger, have less pain, and better posture."

You may have heard the word "core" tossed around, and its importance in regard to exercise. The core is a group of muscles that works in harmony to stabilize your lower back, hips, pelvis, and abdomen. Strong core muscles lead to stability and balance whether you are on the playing field or engaging in the activities of daily living. Strong core muscles also make it easier to do everything from swinging a golf club to getting a can of paint off a high shelf. Poor core strength is good for business—my business, that is. Weak core muscles leave you susceptible to lower back pain, poor posture, and muscle strains.

Exercises

The following exercises were the ones that I suggested Maryanne start with. If you are interested in getting more information on additional exercises, there are many books and videos that are available. Browse through them and find one or two that are a good fit for you. If you are having trouble visualizing what a particular exercise looks like, there is a good chance that you can find a YouTube video that shows it. Also, consider hiring a trainer to get you started. They not only will be able to show you how to exercise properly but will also help you to avoid possible injuries from doing too much or performing the exercises incorrectly.

Crunch with legs on an exercise ball or chair

In this exercise, you lie on your back with your legs on an exercise ball or a chair so that your knees are at a 90-degree angle. Place your hands across your chest or behind your head. If you do put your hands behind your head, be careful not to pull on your neck. (Behind your head is more difficult because it places more weight distally—that is, away from the center of your body.)

Keeping your chin tucked, lift only your shoulder blades off the ground, then slowly lower yourself and return to the starting position. Next, turn your head to the left and again lift up with only your shoulder blades leaving the ground and slowly return to the starting position. Repeat to the right side and continue alternating left, center, and right. Start slow with fifteen repetitions and gradually build up to more.

Leg Lift

Begin by lying on your back with your legs extended out straight. Sliding your hands under your buttocks will help to create stability and support your low back. Slowly lift your legs off the ground about twelve inches. If this is difficult, start with one leg at a time until you are strong enough to do both. Hold for one to two seconds and then return to starting position. Do as many as you can for thirty seconds then rest for fifteen seconds. Start with a minute and slowly work your way up to three minutes.

Bird Dog

Begin on all fours with your hands under your shoulders and knees under your hips. Keep your back straight and your head in line with your spine. Extend one arm and hold for fifteen seconds. Return to the starting position. Then extend the opposite leg and hold for fifteen seconds. Return to the starting position. Then repeat using the opposite arm and leg. At first, you may feel wobbly, but as you continue to perform the exercise, you will be able to hold the position effortlessly. Once you are able to hold the position, extend one arm and the opposite leg at the same time and again hold for fifteen seconds. Work your way up to five repetitions on each side.

Modified Side Plank

Begin by lying on your side with your arm bent, resting the weight of your body on your elbow, and the lower part of your arm underneath your shoulder. Knees should be bent with your torso in a straight line. Begin by lifting your body up so that the weight is on your knees and elbow. Keep your body as straight as possible. Hold for thirty seconds. Work up to five repetitions on each side.

Wood Chop

Begin by standing with your legs slightly wider than your shoulders, while holding a medicine ball or something that weighs about four to six pounds. Raise the ball over your head, bend the knees, and move the hips back while lowering the ball. Arms stay straight as you lower the ball to approximately your knees. It is important that your knees are in line with your toes and not in front of them, otherwise it puts too much strain on the back. Repeat the exercise fifteen times and work your way up to three sets.

You don't need a degree in exercise physiology or have to understand what's going on in your body to exercise well. I do recommend
having a session or two with a trainer if you are going to lift weights
and don't have any experience. Just a few pointers on positioning and
how to use the equipment can save you time and significantly reduce
your chance of getting injured. Most gyms have a session that they
offer free as part of joining. If you are joining a gym, make sure you

take advantage of this opportunity and inquire about what services they can provide.

If yoga is something that interests you, I often suggest that you find a class for beginners initially. The instructor will usually take more time with you to make sure you understand the pose and that you do it right. If time or money poses an issue, consider getting yoga DVDs that you can do at home. Once you have the basics down, they provide you the opportunity to do it whenever you want without having to drive somewhere.

Hiking and taking walks, whether in your neighborhood, mountains, or beach can be a great source of exercise, not to mention it is great to be outside in nature. Recently, I went hiking in the mountains with friends, and despite the fact that I do some form of exercise virtually every day, I found I was sore the next day in both my arms and legs because I was using muscles in ways that I normally don't. I was pulling myself up on rocks, climbing over logs, lifting branches, and hopping across stones in the river. Anytime you can engage your whole body in the exercise process, you are strengthening your core, which assists in creating better balance and coordination.

When I was doing research for this book, I came across several articles about the need and importance of taking it slowly with seniors to make a lasting change. Truthfully, I found it offensive to single out seniors. We all need to take it slowly when we are making life changes that we want to last. I can't tell you the number of people whom I have cared for over the years who get all excited about making changes—starting off with exuberant energy, exercising almost every day, eating salads, counting calories, having substantial change occur—and then they burn out and go right back to where they began, sometimes even worse than where they started.

I encourage you to find the easiest way to incorporate exercises into your life. For some, that means buying exercise equipment for their home. For others, it may mean joining a gym convenient to work so that they can exercise at lunch or before or after work. Consider asking a friend to start a walking program with you or going to an exercise class together. It is harder not to show up when you know that someone is waiting for you. It is also more fun to work out together.

To make long lasting life changes, you must adapt them into your life. They have to become your life. Otherwise, it is still something that you do instead of who you are. In my life, exercise is not just something that I make myself do to be healthy. It is who I am. I play golf and tennis with my friends. My daughter and I might ride bikes to work and school because it's a beautiful day, not because it gets exercise out of the way for the day.

The same thing is true with food. If you are someone who doesn't eat healthily or doesn't really know what that means, then the likelihood of having lasting changes in your diet by radically changing everything are slim to none—this happens because you are in a battle with yourself. It stands to reason that, one way or the other, you will be on the losing end. You will either overeat or make bad choices, or you will constantly be suffering from loss because you are depriving yourself of the foods you want. There is a balance, but more important than a balance is finding the place where you love yourself enough to want to give yourself the nourishment that you need both emotionally and physically.

I believe the best and the worst thing is that once you know something, you cannot un-know it. Once you experience how something impacts you, it becomes a constant background of awareness that doesn't go away. This can and often does become the impetus for change. The important thing is that you don't use this information to punish yourself for what you are not doing. Many times when people start a self-care program, whether in diet or exercise, and fail to follow it through, they punish themselves with self-talk such as "I'm such a slacker" or "I never follow through with anything." These messages we tell ourselves become our reality. Think for a moment about the messages that you send yourself. Are they encouraging or self-defeating before you even start? Know that finding your way may take a little time and a good bit of trial and error. The error is there simply for you to know what doesn't work for you, not that you couldn't do it.

Conclusion

See It, Believe It, Feel It, Become It!

Throughout this book, we have discussed many aspects that must be addressed in order for you to truly be living the life you were meant to live as your authentic self. We considered this from a spirit, mind, and body approach with the belief that if you are able to deal with it early on when your spirit is trying to get your attention, it will decrease the likelihood that the effects will end up in your body. We have reflected on the importance of being able to follow the threads of your life in order to find your destiny. Additionally, we have looked at the effect that stress has on your brain and your ability to make changes in your life and the many ways in which you can calm down the noise in your brain. Lastly, we looked at the significance of what you eat, how you sleep, and what you do for exercises.

Each of the topics that we have explored throughout this book are important in their own right, but the real magic happens when you put all the pieces together by seeing, feeling, believing, and, finally, becoming your authentic self. Whether you consider this from a spirit, mind, body approach or a body, mind, spirit approach, the goal is finding balance and living in your sweet spot. The irony is not lost on me that the mind is in the middle of it all, no matter what route you take, because what you think plays a significant role in what is created.

This is sort of like the "fake it 'til you make it" concept but not totally. Sometimes the process happens without our even being aware that we have gone through the steps and sometimes it is a deliberate step-by-step process.

Either way, it's almost impossible to step into your authentic self without being able to visualize what and who you are and clearly say I want. Whether it's I want to be a musician, a doctor, a mother, a writer, or anything else, you first have to conceive of it and what it might look and feel like in order to create it. It may not look exactly the way you thought it would when you get there, though often it is better than you could have imagined, but it is, nonetheless, a critical step in the process.

Feeling it involves getting each and every one of your cells fully engaged in the creation. It is the way we bridge the gap from being where we are to where we want to be. In this state, every subtle nuance becomes important.

Believing is trusting that you may not know how it will happen and surrendering to the fact that it will happen. This can often be the most difficult step because our minds and egos will get in the way and forever want to tell us that it is impossible or we don't deserve it.

Once you have put all the pieces together, stepping into and becoming yourself is the icing on the cake. It doesn't mean there still isn't work to be done, but there is usually unbridled joy along with a sense of ease and gratitude that makes everything worthwhile.

One woman I know wanted to find her dream home. To begin the creation, she sat down and wrote out everything that she desired in her home. She wanted a bungalow-style house with a yard and at least one fireplace, a garage, and many other specific details. She went further to describe in detail the type and feel of neighborhood she wanted to live in. She decided how far she was willing to drive from work, as well as what kind of neighbors she wanted and just about every other detail she could think of. When it came time to buy her home, she related all the details to her agent, who, at first, seemed a little overwhelmed. At the end of the second outing, he took her to a neighborhood that she loved but totally knew she couldn't afford.

"What are we doing here" she asked incredulously, as they drove down the old oak-lined streets.

"There's a house here that will be a little bit of a stretch financially, but I think you'll be able to swing it, and it meets all your needs," he said.

"Seriously? Are you kidding? I have always wanted to live here. I love this neighborhood!"

She fell in love with the house as soon as they pulled up in front of it. As they meandered from room to room, she found herself picturing where the furniture would go and how she would use each of the rooms. She fully embraced the feeling of what it would be like to live there. She put a contract on the house immediately and, with a little negotiation, was living in the house of her dreams about a month later.

What she had forgotten was that when she was in college, she frequently rode her bike through this neighborhood and would allow herself to dream. She would picture herself living in one of the beautiful homes and imagine what it would be like to live there. She would think about what the neighbors would be like and how it would feel to take walks on these beautiful tree-lined streets. She had totally forgotten all of this until she took the first evening walk and was flooded with remembering all the thoughts and feelings she used to have about living there. "Hmm," she thought to herself, "There just might be something to this creating stuff."

Another woman I know really wanted to be a successful practitioner. Although making money would be helpful, the real success for her was the joy of being able to be of service to the patients she felt privileged to care for. She fully understood what value there was in accessing feelings as way to bridge the gap from where you are to where you want to be. She passed all of her boards, and in the early days of opening her practice, she spent several hours each week swimming laps at the local Salvation Army pool.

Throughout each hour while she swam, she would picture in her mind and create the feeling in her body of having a successful practice. She visualized people getting well and felt the feeling of serving in a busy, full schedule and helping many people with all types of issues. She would visualize herself moving from room to room, focusing on each person's needs as they came and went. She also would picture herself donating time by going back out into the community and giving back.

She would imagine what it might feel like to go home each night after a fulfilling day of work and be filled with gratitude knowing that she was able to live the life she wanted to live. In just a few short months, she was living that very life and she continues to this day. She would tell you emphatically that this part of the creation process was critical to her creating the life she wanted.

Another woman related a story about how she created the office that she practiced in. While in school, one of the courses that she was required to take involved creating a binder that contained everything that one needed to a go out into the real world and create a practice. This meant that you had to pick a city, write to the chamber of commerce, gather all the demographics and decipher them, and decide where you would put your practice. Additionally, you were required to decide everything from how much you would charge to the size of your office, as well as a detailed drawing of the layout right down to where the outlets were located. You then had to prepare a proposal for a loan at a bank.

Needless to say, it was a very extensive project and took an entire semester. Unfortunately, students often copy information and data from an upper classman when taking this class, but this woman actually enjoyed the process and found it helped her to focus on what she wanted in a practice.

After the semester, she passed her information on to a friend so he could look at what she had done and understand how the process worked. It was about a year later when it was time for her to start her practice, and she asked him to return the project so she could review all that she had done and create a real proposal for the bank.

It was decided that he would bring the information to her at the new office that she had rented that day, as he was as eager to see it and she was to show it off. She excitedly showed him every nook and cranny of the empty space that would very soon house her practice.

She thanked him as he left and sat down on the floor in the dusty vacant office and began to sift through the information he had returned to her. As she examined each piece, she came across the original floor plan that she had created a year and a half ago. She stared at it for a long time and had that eerie feeling that she was missing something.

She turned the floor plan sideways and looked at it again. It was then that a prickly feeling spread throughout her whole body as she realized that the floor plan in her hand was the exact floor plan of the office she had just rented, right down to where the kids' waiting room was located. She, too, knew the value of seeing, feeling, believing, and becoming, which is why it was so important to her to do the project by herself. Many years later, she is still successfully practicing in that location.

You see, I know the stories of all of these women personally. Each of these stories is mine. Each one of these things happened because I intentionally saw it, felt it, believed it, and became it, and you can too. I invite you to empower yourself to create whatever it is that your heart truly desires and step wholeheartedly into your authentic self.

I look forward to sharing more information about each of these concepts and the process of creating in my next book:

See, Feel, Believe, Become.

Bibliography

Ahadi, Batool, and Saeed Ariapooran. 2009. "Role of Self and Other Forgiveness in Predicting Depression and Suicide Ideation of Divorcees." *Journal of Applied Sciences* 9(19): 3598–3601.

Berry, J. W., and Everett Worthington. 2001. "Forgiveness, Relationship Quality, Stress While Imagining Relationship Events, and Physical and Mental Health." *Journal of Counseling Psychology* 48: 447–455.

Brown, Brené. 2012. *Daring Greatly: How the Courage to Be Vulnerable Transforms the Way We Live, Love, Parent, and Lead.* Los Angeles: Gotham.

Childre, Doc, and Rollin McCraty. 2002. *The Appreciative Heart: The Psychophysiology of Positive Emotions and Optimal Functioning.* Boulder Creek, CA: Institute of HeartMath.

Danese, Andrea, Carmine M. Pariante, Avshalom Caspi, Alan Taylor, and Richie Poulton. 2007. "Childhood Maltreatment Predicts Adult Inflammation in a Life-Course Study." *Proceedings of the National Academy of Sciences of the United States of America* 104(4): 1319–1324.

Elliott, B. A. 2011. "Forgiveness Therapy: A Clinical Intervention for Chronic Disease." *Journal of Religion and Health* 50(2): 240–247.

"Five for 2005: Five Reasons to Forgive." 2005. *Harvard Women's Health Watch* 12 (5): 1–3.

Jacques, Renne. 2013. "These Disturbing Fast Food Truths Will Make You Reconsider Your Lunch." *The Huffington Post*, November 20.http://www.huffingtonpost.com/2013/11/20/fast-food-truths_n_4296243.html.

Lavie, Carl J. 2014. *The Obesity Paradox: When Thinner Means Sicker and Heavier Means Healthier.* New York: Hudson Street Press.

Luskin, Fredric. 2003. *Forgive for Good.* New York: HarperOne.

McCullough, M. E., J. A. Tsang, and R. A. Emmons. 2004. "Gratitude in Intermediate Affective Terrain: Links of Grateful Moods to Individual Differences and Daily Emotional Experience." *Journal of Personality and Social Psychology* 86: 295–309.

Murck, Harald, Alex Steiger, Ralf M. Frieboes, and Irina A. Antonijevic. 2006. "Pituitary Adenylate Cyclase-Activing Peptide Affects Homeostatic Sleep Regulation in Healthy Young Men." *American Journal of Physiology – Endocrinology and Metabolism* 292(3): 853–857.

Neff, Kristin. 2011. *Self-Compassion: The Proven Power of Being Kind to Yourself.* New York: William Morrow.

Patil, Harsal R., James H. O'Keefe, Carl J. Lavie, Antony Magalski, Robert A. Vogel, and Peter A. McCullough. 2012. "Cardiovascular Damage Resulting From Chronic Excessive Endurance Exercise." *Missouri Medicine* 109(4). 312–321.

Sansone, R. A., and L. A. Sansone. 2010. "Gratitude and Well-Being: the Benefits of Appreciation." *Psychiatry* 7(11): 18–22.

Seybold, K. S., P. C. Hill, J. K. Neumann, and D. S. Chi. 2001. "Physiological and Psychological Correlates of Forgiveness." *Journal of Psychological Christianity* 20: 250–259.

Tierney, John. 2011. "A Serving of Gratitude May Save the Day." *New York Times*, November 21. http://www.nytimes.com/2011/11/22/science/a-serving-of-gratitude-brings-healthy-dividends.html.

Watkins, P. C., D. L. Grimm, T. Stone, and R. L. Kolts. 2003. "Gratitude and Happiness: Development of a Measure of Gratitude, and Relationships with Subjective Well-Being." *Social Behavior and Personality* 31: 431–451.

Wen, Chi Pang, Jackson Pui Man Wai, Min Kuang Tsai, Yi Chen Yang, Ting Yuan David Cheng, Meng-Chih Lee, Hui Ting Chan, Chwen Keng Tsao, Shan Pou Tsai, and Xifeng Wu. 2011. "Minimum Amount of Physical Activity For Reduced Mortality and Extended Life Expectancy: A Prospective Cohort Study." *The Lancet* 378(9798): 1244–1253.

Worthington, Everett. (2005). *The Power of Forgiveness.* New York: Brunner-Routledge.

About the Author

Dr. Pat Gibson is the founder and director of the Gibson Chiropractic Clinic, P.C., located just outside of Atlanta. She brings thirty plus years of experience to her multidimensional practice, incorporating a three-pronged approach to assist each individual in correcting whatever imbalances are present. She utilizes nutritional supplements along with diet and lifestyle changes to correct for organ and chemical imbalances, chiropractic care to address structural imbalance, and emotionally-based body work to help clients get at that not-so-conscious piece that is demanding attention.

Additionally, she has designed and facilitated workshops on the "science of happiness," which assists individuals in getting to the core of what prevents them from living a balanced life with joy and passion, as well as giving them tools to create change.

Dr. Gibson has helped thousands of patients to heal core imbalances in their lives and bodies. Her unique style and compassion engenders a rare sensitivity with each person she encounters.